MW00770008

"We need Gospel-centered women in business and ministry these days . . . women who will champion us and encourage us, and who will also give us truth. I could not be more grateful for Somer and Michelle, and how they use their voices to do just that. You will love this book, and they will love you through it!"

—Jess Connolly, author of *You Are the Girl for the Job* and *Breaking Free from Body Shame*

"Michelle and Somer have crafted a book that is compassionate about all the pressures women carry every day as well as foundationally inspiring, calling women to live vibrantly and purposefully with God as their focus. Be inspired and refreshed through this wonderful book and find practical ways forward to order your life."

—Sally Clarkson, beloved author, podcaster of *At Home With Sally*, and best friend of her four adult children

"God has called every woman to do important work in this world. I love the countercultural, Gospel-centered message of She Works His Way, and I know you will too. This is the book for every working woman!"

—Alli Worthington, bestselling author, business coach, and entrepreneur

"An excellent, encouraging, Gospel-centric book. The world is waiting in eager expectation for more women to work and live in the way of the Way. Michelle and Somer will show you how."

—Jordan Raynor, national bestselling author of *Called to Create* and *Master of One*

"Do you know what I love the very most about Michelle Myers and Somer Phoebus? They continually point their community of women back to Jesus and His Word. *She Works His Way* is no exception. In this book, you will be inspired and challenged to see your work in a whole new way while ultimately encouraged to cling to God first and foremost. Every working woman, whether full-time, part-time, at home, or in ministry, needs the fresh perspective found in these pages!"

—Ruth Schwenk, founder of TheBetterMom.com, co-host of *Rootlike Faith* podcast, and co-author of *Settle My Soul*

"Do you struggle with getting things done without coming undone, despite every slick hack, clever app, or piece of 'life balance' advice you've tried? Perhaps it is time to stop trying and start trusting instead. Michelle and Somer help you discover the secret to successfully managing the tension between work tasks, home life, and your many relationships. It's not accomplished by frantically bouncing between them all, trying to make them obediently fall in line. It's achieved when you learn how to put Christ at the center of your daily life and allow everything else to fall into place. This practical and biblical resource will empower you to do just that. Highly recommended!"

—Karen Ehman, *New York Times* bestselling author, Proverbs 31 Ministries speaker, wife, and mom of five

"Michelle and Somer are, simply put, a great team. They're a trusted voice in a culture where no one really knows who they can trust. We love their hearts and we need their message, especially now! We can't wait to see how God uses this book."

—Clayton and Sharie King, co-founders of Crossroads Events and Clayton King Ministries

"In a world riddled with self-help and #girlboss content, I wholeheartedly recommend this book if you're hoping for a guide that clearly articulates how to channel your ambition for the Kingdom—not for yourself. In *She Works His Way*,

Michelle and Somer strike the perfect balance between conviction, compassion, and actionable items—a must read."

—Amanda Tress, CEO of FASTer Way to Fat Loss

"In a day and time when hustle is glorified as holy, it is no wonder that as women we find ourselves empty. We've been taught to believe, but no one showed us how to build . . . not from our to-do lists, but from a place of destiny anchored in eternity. In *She Works His Way*, Michelle and Somer do a brilliant job of walking us through what it means to truly operate in, from, and for the blessing of God. A timely, bold, and beautiful read."

—Marshawn Evans Daniels, Godfidence Coach®,
TV personality, reinvention strategist for women,
and founder of SheProfits.com

"In work, it's so easy to drift to the world's way of doing things. The lies are subtle and the expectations are strong. That's why it has been transformative to learn about the She Works His Way approach from Michelle and Somer over the last six years. What a gift to now have that message distilled into this powerful book for all women to read!"

—Valerie Woerner, prayer journal creator,
owner of Val Marie Paper, and author of
Pray Confidently and Consistently

"She Works His Way is a message for such a time as this. Women now more than ever need to be reminded of the power and presence of Jesus, the mission we've been gifted in the kingdom, and the way God works in and through our lives. This book will propel women into a life of holy purpose, keeping what's good and Gospel-centered at the forefront of their lives."

—Alexandra Hoover, author, ministry leader,
and Bible teacher

she works His way

she works His way

A PRACTICAL GUIDE FOR DOING WHAT MATTERS MOST IN A GET-THINGS-DONE WORLD

MICHELLE MYERS
AND SOMER PHOEBUS

Published by Bethany House Publishers
11400 Hampshire Avenue South
Bloomington, Minnesota 55438
www.bethanyhouse.com

Bethany House Publishers is a division of
Baker Publishing Group, Grand Rapids, Michigan

Library of Congress Cataloging-in-Publication Data

Names: Myers, Michelle, author. | Phoebus, Somer, author.

Title: She works His way : a practical guide for doing what matters most in a get-things-done world / Michelle Myers and Somer Phoebus.

Description: Minneapolis, Minnesota : Bethany House, [2021] | Includes bibliographical references.

Identifiers: LCCN 2021015653 | ISBN 9780764239731 (casebound) | ISBN 9780764237690 (paperback) | ISBN 9781493433544 (ebook)

Subjects: LCSH: Christian women—Religious life. | Work-life balance. | Women employees—Religious life. | Time management—Religious aspects—Christianity. | Simplicity—Religious aspects—Christianity.

Classification: LCC BV4527 .M945 2021 | DDC 248.8/43—dc23

LC record available at https://lccn.loc.gov/2021015653

Cover design by Kara Klontz

Baker Publishing Group publications use paper produced from sustainable forestry practices and post-consumer waste whenever possible.

21 22 23 24 25 26 27 7 6 5 4 3 2 1

From Michelle:

James, your sacrificial leadership is a huge reason why this book exists—thank you. Also, consider this my unofficial citation of you because otherwise, footnotes would have gotten out of control. Your impact on me is woven in every word here.

Noah, Cole + Shea, I thought the worldwide pandemic that brought you home from school was going to make writing this book more difficult, but as I heard you playing outside my office while I wrote, it only made what I was writing more important. So much of what you see here are my prayers for you as you grow in Him. I love you the most, Team Myers.

From Somer:

Kent, your quiet, chill wisdom has been overwhelmingly loud to me. You've taught me more than anyone. I've never been so glad that we share the same last name *(as weird as it is)* because it's only fair you get credit here too.

Kennedi and Lizzie, writing a book designed to encourage working women to pursue Jesus above all else while you were both at the brink of adulthood making major life decisions was a gift only God could have orchestrated. These words aren't just dedicated to you, they're written to you. Just know I do not care in what capacity you choose to do it, but I care wholeheartedly that you spend every ounce of energy you have serving Jesus. Thank you for being my biggest inspiration.

Contents

Foreword

Michelle Myers and Somer Phoebus are focused, energetic women who get a lot of things done.

But do not let their production level fool you. They are fueled by more than career ambition, passion, and fruit-and-nut power bars.

Jesus is their Source.

The first time I met this super-duo, I felt an immediate connection to them, despite their ability to wear cute overalls, which I do not share. Their joy is contagious. Their warmth, endearing. Michelle and Somer are the women you want in your corner—girls' girls, always cheering you on. That same spirit is felt in their She Works HIS Way ministry, and now in the pages of this book—a kinship to the struggle of every woman who has things she wants to do but doesn't want to sacrifice family on the altar of her goals and dreams.

They've been there, which makes them the perfect women to write this book.

I have been there too.

My daughter is now eighteen, but I'll never forget the day when she was about eight and walked into my office, innocently pronouncing a sentence that broke my heart: "I wish you weren't one of those worker moms." I'm sure she just wanted my attention in that moment and didn't want to share it with my computer screen. But all I heard was utter disappointment that I wasn't the mom she wanted. In the one job I had always dreamed of doing well, I had obviously failed.

That moment was a real catalyst for me. It was around then that I began to truly give God my tug-of-war between hustle and home. That was when peace replaced both overworking and guilt.

Turns out that when Jesus is over everything, a lot of our daily complications get sorted out.

I never was a classroom mom, but I'm happy to report that over time I became a woman, wife, and mother who did the work God called her to, His way—despite my very human, very regular life struggles. It's one of the reasons I so strongly believe in the message of She Works HIS Way. The anthem of freedom it carries is one I've found beautifully possible.

If you are looking for a wise approach to productivity without frenzy, you've found the perfect book.

And in case you are still skeptical such a way exists, please allow me to say this last thing: Jesus would not call you to do work that would exhaust and deplete you, or demand that you sacrifice the abundant life He has promised. If that exhaustion is your reality right now, I'm particularly thrilled you're reading this book so you can be encouraged in a better way.

In a culture where everyone has an opinion and people are eager to sell you on their methods, know that there is but one tried and true model of success.

Jesus, first, always.

There is but One Way—*the Way, the Truth, and the Life.*

I'm so grateful it is the Way in which Michelle and Somer are leading us.

—Lisa Whittle, bestselling author of *Jesus Over Everything*

1

His Story

Our Story

Michelle + Somer

Culture says: Life balance is the solution.

God says: I am the Solution.

We (Michelle and Somer) have seen firsthand the deep desire women have for a "balanced" life. We've felt it ourselves. But we are pushing back on that approach because, although balance can be good for us, it isn't God's best for us. (Believe us—between the two of us, we've tried *everything*!)

And if you think about it, what does the word *balance* imply anyway? Usually some form of perfection—and we all know how pursuing perfection tends to go. So we're here to take the modern-day mantra that the solution is a balanced life and test it against what God's Word says.

Women are simultaneously striving to be who God says they are and who the world says they should be. That's not balance, that's *bondage*. And it's happening far too often.

We're all continuously exposed to the enemy's lies, which he often cleverly disguises as half-truths. At any turn, we are just as likely to encounter a deceptive false teacher as we are a well-meaning friend with a strong attachment to a flawed opinion. Not to mention, we have to deal with our own weak flesh and deceitful hearts. We're not living in a world with merely the extremes of good and evil to navigate. This life requires us to discern the difference between what is merely good and what is actually of God.

It's a confusing and frustrating place to exist . . . if our focus does not remain where it belongs.

That's what we're here to do: help you to refocus. We're going to expose culture's lies (especially the well-dressed, socially acceptable ones) and elevate God's truth above all else.

"But seek first the kingdom of God and His righteousness, and all these things will be provided for you," Matthew 6:33 HCSB.

If you take nothing else away from this book, remember this:

Better life balance is not the solution. *Order* is. We were divinely designed to put God first.

Deep down in the depths of our soul, we crave Him. And He won't tolerate being second because He can't. He's God. So it would make sense that if your priority order is mixed up or inverted, you'll feel anxious, discontent, and aimless. And to escape those feelings, you'll try to work harder, do more, and be better in all the ways the world tells you to because that is the promise culture makes us: More self-care, self-study, ambition, and all the good vibes you can muster up will bring you the happiness you desire, the success you deserve, and the balance you're desperate for.

But we're calling their bluff because "from him and through him and to him are all things. To him be glory forever. Amen."[1] Everything starts, is sustained by, and will eventually end with God.

The world is trying *so* hard to convince you that you can do it all, be it all, and have it all. And part of you really wants to believe it. After all, you are a strong, smart, and capable woman.

Better life balance is not the solution. *Order* is. We were divinely designed to put God first.

But you also know you are not stronger, smarter, or more capable than God.

And while we *know* that's true, the real question is: Do we *live* like it's true?

Dependence on God is the foundation for following Him. That's why we must constantly remind ourselves that as believers, self-sufficiency is a deficiency. **Because you can't live in a way that is both God-dependent and self-sufficient.**

Proverbs 3:5 makes a distinction between the two, instructing us, "Trust in the Lord with all your heart, and do not lean on your own understanding." Trusting the Lord with all of our hearts also means we refuse to lean on our own understanding.

There is strength in being a determined hard worker—which we're certain you are. But being a hard worker without depending on God can transform this strength into a blind spot. If we're simply getting things done, but neglecting to do what matters, the world may call us super productive, but the truth is that we're actually spiritually lazy. (*Yikes!*)

Only what we do for Christ is what lasts. Everything else fades away.

Maybe you absolutely love your job. You are so passionate about your mission, and you can't believe this is what you get

1. Romans 11:36.

to do. But you know you struggle with workaholic tendencies. *You belong here.*

Maybe you're currently working a difficult job and you spend your morning commute dreading the day ahead and your evening commute begging God to change your circumstance—but He has asked you to stay. *You belong here.*

Employer or employee? *You belong here.*

Paid or unpaid? *You belong here.*

Secular work or traditional ministry? *You belong here.*

At the peak of your career, retired, just getting started or even still in school? Say it with us this time: *You belong here.*

Our world needs women who work His way in our schools, hospitals, courtrooms, offices, churches, hair salons, studios, network marketing companies, spas, real estate agencies, gyms, stores, factories, corporations, and government buildings.

We need women who work His way serving as administrative assistants, CEOs, volunteers, creatives, and entrepreneurs, as well as in middle management and in every single support role that exists between.

What connects our mission isn't that we have a common career, but that we serve the same Savior. He designs us uniquely and scatters us to diverse places, but He gives us a unified mission:

> Go therefore and make disciples of all nations, baptizing them in the name of the Father and of the Son and of the Holy Spirit, teaching them to observe all that I have commanded you. And behold, I am with you always, to the end of the age.
>
> Matthew 28:19–20

And while this verse is most commonly used in the context of a short-term trip or full-time missionaries, this is not a short-term verse for one vocation; this is an everyday calling for all who follow Jesus.

The mission field isn't some faraway destination or somewhere God may send us someday. His mission field for you is wherever He has you.

Your home is a mission field.

Your job is a mission field.

As a believer, the mission field is anywhere you go.

The She Works HIS Way Story

She Works HIS Way didn't begin as a brand or a book. We didn't have a social media account or a five-year plan. We certainly didn't have a logo, a membership, a partnership with YouVersion for daily devotions, a conference, or a website, as we do now.

It started with a few friends who loved Jesus fiercely, took our assignments as wives and moms seriously, and felt called to use our God-given gifts, talents, and abilities in our jobs. We met once a week at 5 AM on Google Hangouts.

Our conversations varied in topic, but we were consistent in sharpening one another as Christ-followers, wives, moms, and professionals. We asked each other hard questions. It even got uncomfortable at times. But being uncomfortable was better than the alternative of being seduced by the world to the point of becoming so "successful" and so wrapped up in our careers that we would be irrelevant in God's mission and at home.

We were watching it happen, and not to just anyone, but to women we really respected. Marriages and homes were unraveling. Priorities were shifting. And we knew that if it could happen to them, it could just as easily happen to us.

Praise God, we realized we couldn't rely on the strength of our own flesh, but we knew that to fulfill His purpose for our lives we needed His strength and the community of others who were following Jesus closely.

As each of us made our way through business training and personal development on our own, we realized it was hard to find advice we could fully trust, so we were constantly bringing the content we consumed to one another, asking the same four questions:

Does this keep me dependent on God?

Gifts, talents, and abilities are real, but the One who put them in us is more real. We want to be women who rely on God, not on our gifting.

Does this keep me dedicated to my family?

Jobs will likely fluctuate throughout our lives, but we never have to question the assignments God has given only to us. Our family roles offer us our greatest opportunity for significance. In a world that is constantly trying to define success for us as "bigger" and "better," we need to be reminded of the high calling and the unique opportunity God has given us at home.

Does this make me effective at work?

Excellence matters to God, so excellence should matter to us. But it takes more than excellence or skill to be effective. Being effective requires open eyes and open hearts. Being effective requires love. Being effective means we must redefine success as obedience to God. Nothing more. Nothing less.

Does this hinder my commitment to the Gospel?

We live in the age of the side hustle, automation, and monetization—and the notion that more work must be better. Given the fact that technology makes us always accessible, work could occupy so much of your life and brain space that you have no margin left to simply be available to those God puts in your life, let alone serve your local church.

But God doesn't ask for our leftovers. He demands our firstfruits. To be honest, how we live this truth is probably the quickest way to determine whether we've joined His agenda or are attempting to use His name to push our own.

Today, our ministry calls these four questions the *SWHW filter*, and it's still the criteria for the content we create and promote.

After meeting for over a year on Google Hangouts, we felt God's prompting to invite more women to join us. Michelle started an Instagram account to share what God was showing us, and we were quickly blown away by how much women craved this conversation. Six months or so later we moved to an email list, and about a year after that we launched an online membership community.

God doesn't ask for our leftovers. He demands our firstfruits.

We also have an app, an annual conference, a growing presence of trained local leaders in cities scattered around the globe, and now—a book. We continue to remain in awe of what God continues to do with this mission that started as friends holding one another accountable to work for the glory of the Lord and the good of others, and we believe He's just getting started.

Meet Michelle

I'm so grateful you're here! I'm Michelle, and I believe that in order for us to talk about some of the hard (but so important!) truths we're going to unpack inside these pages, we have to be able to get honest with each other, and we need to become real friends *fast*.

So here's a speed-dating version of what you really need to know about me that will get us to "talk-like-best-friends" level.

I don't remember a time in my life when I wasn't an approval junkie. Even in elementary school, I wondered whether my teachers were mad at me if I didn't get an A. As I entered middle school, I looked at the way other girls dressed and the way the popular kids talked, and I caved to the pressure to be cool.

I wasn't boy crazy at as young an age as many of my friends, but I was once I had a boyfriend. From high school on, male approval became a critical part of how I viewed my worth.

Approval was the root of my four-year eating disorder.

Approval was why, middle school through college, I was frequently changing myself to act like whoever I was around.

And approval is *still* the reason why, without the appropriate boundaries and accountability, I have a natural bent toward being a workaholic.

Gaining the approval of others wasn't just a struggle, a battle, a conflict, or any other more palatable word I may have used as an attempt to mask the severity of my reality.

Others' approval wasn't just something that I *liked*. I was *living* for it. It is what determined whether I had a good day or a bad day. Approval is what I would look to as the solution when I was sad or disappointed.

So almost a decade ago, as a young pastor's wife with a toddler and another baby boy on the way, I found myself in a job where there was no limit to the amount of money I could make, the hours I could work, or the recognition I could receive. I also had a lot of freedom in terms of flexibility in my hours and even the ability to incorporate my faith into my work.

The rational part of my brain knows that sounds like a dream job, and honestly, in some ways it seemed like everything was working out more perfectly than I had ever planned. But inside, I felt an unsettled, familiar tug in my spirit: My work was beginning to take Christ's place as the main source of my joy, my worth, my contentment, and my purpose.

I had been down that road, and I did not want to go back. I knew how to go through the motions of my Christian life—sing the right songs, quote the right verses, and attend every service and Bible study offered—but when it came down to how I was living my everyday life, my thoughts and actions proved I was worshiping human opinion instead of the God who made me.

As you look back on your life, do you see areas where you hungered for others' approval?

For me, the problem manifested itself almost my entire life, and it wasn't that I didn't realize it or never attempted to fix it. I tried to stress *less* about my grades. I tried to care *less* about boys paying attention to me, my appearance, and what others thought about me in general.

But none of my attempts to need approval *less* ever worked long-term.

Approval was my idol. A more painful way to put it is that approval was my god. It's uncomfortable to say it that way. If you're like me, it's much easier to call something a *struggle* than to call it a *sin*. But when we don't call sin what it is, it's much easier to overlook the idols in our lives.

Tim Keller puts it this way: "An idol is something that we look to for things that only God can give."[1]

Maybe approval isn't your idol, but perhaps it's one of these:

Money	**Control**
Success	**Stuff**

Or even just . . . **Self.**

Money doesn't make a good god . . . because money gives false security. God is your Provider.

Success isn't a good god . . . because typically, when we chase success the world's way, we end up failing where it matters most.

Control isn't a good god . . . because God's in control, not you.

Stuff isn't a good god . . . because you came into this world with nothing, and you will be taking nothing with you when you leave it.[2]

And *you* certainly don't make a good god . . . because (even though I like you, and you're pretty great!) you are *still* a sinner in need of a Savior.

Filling our hearts with the love of our Father, picking up our cross, denying ourselves, following Jesus, and daily choosing to live in the power of the Holy Spirit—*that* is the only way to break free from the idols of this world. Otherwise, we'll spend our lives moving from idol to idol, rather than making God the sole Recipient of our worship and the primary Object of our affection.

Attempts to *reduce* our earthly idols never work. Idols must be *replaced*.

It can't stop at liking Jesus; we must follow Him. Jesus was never meant to be merely an addition to our lives, but to be our firm foundation. That's why I'm so passionate about this message. I'm a fixer, and I feel like I wasted many years of my life trying to use secondary solutions to solve my primary problem. I don't want to waste another second worshiping or living for anything except the God who made me.

Meet Somer

Hey! I'm Somer, a recovering chronic compartmentalizer with a pretty serious addiction to French fries, and I'm really glad you're here.

I'll be honest: I'm a bit worried what your first impression of me is going to be after reading about my worst qualities, but we're all about being real here so if you promise not to give up

2. 1 Timothy 6:7.

on me after this first chapter, I promise not to give up on you over the rest of this book!

My story is a little different from Michelle's. For me it wasn't others' approval I was after as much—I needed to prove myself.

I'm not really sure why. I could probably talk it all out and get to something in my childhood that made me feel like the underdog, but I don't know that it's necessarily beneficial because the bottom line is, it was pride. Pride disguised as ambition and a good work ethic, so it was a little hard to spot and definitely a lot harder to admit.

Well-intentioned sin is *still* sin.

I realized from a very young age that the best way to earn my place and prove that I was the best was to become an absolute pro at compartmentalizing everything in my life. (Another name for that would be *control freak*.)

I took this "skill" into my adult life and made sure to be a good pastor's wife at church, an ambitious businesswoman in my career, the fittest and healthiest trainer in the studio I owned, and a domestic queen/No. 1 soccer mom at home.

And probably, not much to your surprise, it was pretty exhausting.

As time went on, I got really good at switching hats. The strategy of compartmentalizing was proving to be the best way to achieve order and success in my daily life. A folder for work, a folder for kids, a folder for marriage, and a folder for God. It felt like I was running in a relay race in which I would circle around to the finish line only to pass the baton to myself—in a different hat of course.

It wasn't long before I started to feel the weight of things. I remember being asked by a woman for whom I was doing a team training, "How *do* you do it all?!"

I had no idea how to answer her because I was dying a little with every new business venture I couldn't say no to.

Finding the next big opportunity had almost become an obsession. Achievement was important to me. I told myself all of it would eventually glorify God and that's how I justified my pace, my mindset, and my striving. I even called my work *ministry* because as a believer, that's what I was taught to call it.

But I didn't work as though work was my ministry; I worked like my work was my *identity*.

And with work as my identity, I was empty. Emotionally, physically, and spiritually empty.

You see, I knew what it felt like to walk with the Lord, and this was not it. I had a deep discontentment in my soul. It was taking more and more in my career to satisfy me; my mood was directly impacted by my level of productivity, so I began to see the biggest blessings of my life as interruptions rather than as gifts. My work "folder" was stealing time and energy from the *areas* that should have been most protected. Specifically, my family.

Around that time, praise Jesus, I was invited to join three of my working-mom friends for a 5 AM Google Hangout. The goal was two-fold: discipleship and friendship with women who understood me. One of those friends was Michelle.

When we started meeting, I had no idea just how much I needed them.

All of my career, I had been praised for my hustle, my titles, and my accomplishments, but that's not what these friends were praising. That wasn't even the reason they were interested in talking to me!

We started asking each other hard questions and going to God's Word for the answers. And the truth that was being revealed to us was pushing back against most everything we had been taught in the personal development books and in the business world. It wasn't about compartmentalizing or controlling; it was about order.

His order: God *first*, family *second*, and work *third*.

So one night, in my driveway after an extra-busy day of work, I was prompted by the Holy Spirit (and time with these friends of mine at 5 AM) to ask my daughters what they thought about my job. I believe my question was, "Do you girls feel like Mom is too busy for you?" I quickly followed up with, "Do you think I'm on my phone too much?"

Now let me preface their answer with this: I have the kindest, sweetest daughters in the whole world. That might sound like a mom brag, and I guess it kind of is, but you have to know that in order to get this moment. The *last* thing they wanted to do was hurt my feelings.

But they did—in the most kind and gentle way. And I'm so thankful they did!

My oldest hesitantly spoke up: "Mama, we think you're so good at your jobs, but sometimes, we feel bad because we have to interrupt you."

My youngest quickly inserted, "But thank you for making money for our family. I know that's why you're on the phone all of the time, and it's okay."

But it wasn't okay.

Yeah, that was my moment. The moment God used to change everything.

My file system was very flawed. Turns out, compartmentalizing put everything in my hands, not His, and that's a dangerous place for anything to be.

The rest of this book is the story of how we traded the lies of the world for the truth of our loving Father: the lessons we learned that challenged culture's "good things" so that we could find the greatest thing and the foundation that reshaped our desires and reordered our priorities as She Works HIS Way women.

I pray so deeply that when you read this, God meets you exactly where you are—like He met me in my driveway that night. And I pray that He rocks you if you need rocking, comforts you if you need to be comforted, or redirects you if you've lost your way.

But most of all, I pray that He becomes way too big to fit into a folder, and instead He takes His rightful place as the Keeper of everything in your life, the One who holds it all.

What to Expect

Our goal is always to be known for what we're *for*, so we want to encourage you with how God has spoken truth into the struggle you're feeling. We want to equip you with practical ways to put His truth into action. But we do feel a responsibility to warn you when some of today's popular voices and work-based movements have flaws in the foundation that, when followed, can create distance between you and God.

The title of each of the following chapters indicates a daily choice we must make to work His way. The phrase on top is God's desire for us, while the phrase on the bottom is culture's half-truth, a blatant lie, or something that's okay as a result but spiritually dangerous when it becomes our goal. These are not one-time decisions, but daily choices we all make—*directly or indirectly*—some of which lean toward our actions, while others dig further to expose our motives.

Take a quick glance at our conversations to come:

His Way *My Way*	**Obedience** *Success*	**Love** *Skill*
Lose Myself *Find Myself*	**You** *Me*	**Listen** *Be Heard*
Know God *Be Known*	**Relationships** *Achievements*	**Serve** *Lead*

Give	**Approved**
Earn	*Approval*

It's not that everything on the lower line is bad. You won't find any success shaming here. We're not saying that you're automatically evil if the world knows who you are. The question is: *What do you pursue?*

Within each chapter, you'll find:

Biblical foundation: These daily decisions aren't rooted in our opinion or our feelings but grounded in what God's Word says. His wisdom far exceeds human knowledge; it not only fills our heads, but His wisdom also has the power to change our hearts. Mere knowledge can quickly escalate into pride, and God's wisdom humbles our hearts to be more like Him.

Practical application: You can't truly encounter God and stay the same. Jesus changes everything—including how we act on what His Word says. Each chapter includes practical ways to put the principle into practice in everyday life—so we can be doers of the Word and not hearers only.[3]

Prayer: At the conclusion of each chapter, we're including a prayer—a raw, real, kind-of-hurts-to-say-out-loud prayer. Before we take action ourselves, turning to prayer means our first step is pursuing a posture of surrender. Prayer positions us to hear from God. And there's no better advice we can offer as an ending than encouraging you personally into His presence. Don't rush your reading of these prayers. Take the prayers as a starting point and personalize them. Search back through the chapter and look for words you underlined and wrote in the margin. Check the footnotes for supporting Scriptures. Turn what stood out to you into prayers. Prayer is the best catalyst for change because prayer is a transfer of power. Dream with

3. James 1:22.

us about what God can do when His daughters *pray* His truth and *live* His truth through His *power.*

Let's Go

We're coming to you as your spiritual sisters, not as experts. We love you, and we're in the trenches of living in this tension with you. Our goal is not to call you out, but to call you *up*. (Conviction is His job—not ours!) We're not above you, and we do love you.

The book you're holding in your hands is really a conversation—a conversation to counteract culture's way with a Gospel-centered approach to both work and womanhood, for the glory of God and the good of others.

Let's get to work. His way. We're really, *really* grateful you're here.

Rooted in Him and rooting for you,
Michelle + Somer

A Prayer Before You Read

Father, I come to You and confess
That it is all too easy to live my life as a simultaneous attempt
To be all that You created me to be
And all the world expects me to be.

In Jesus' name, I ask for Your help to live my decision
That the dual pursuit ends today.
I'm trading life balance for full surrender.
I want to seek first Your kingdom and Your righteousness;
I trust that You will provide everything else.[4]

Position my heart to hear from You.
Help me to hunger and thirst for righteousness.[5]
Give me discernment when I encounter half-truths and blatant lies.
Do not allow me to be satisfied by counterfeit claims.

God, keep me desperately dependent on You.
Make me relentless in the pursuit of my family's hearts.
Give me open eyes to remain effective in my work.
And daily, give me opportunities to live out my commitment to the Gospel.

Reveal to me any idols that have taken Your place,
And don't merely reduce my affection for them, Lord,
But replace my affection for them with an unquenchable desire for You.
Set my mind on things above, not earthly things.[6]

4. Matthew 6:33.
5. Matthew 5:6.
6. Colossians 3:2.

As I'm reading pages in this book,
I'm begging You to speak to me, God.
Convict me and correct me.
Encourage me and equip me.
Show me and shape me.
Change me and use me.
I'm all in for Your kingdom cause.

Soften my heart.
Open my eyes.
Give me willing hands.
My life is Yours.
I no longer live, but Christ lives in me.[7]
I'm picking up my cross and following You,
Today and every day after.[8]
I love You, and I trust You.

Amen.

7. Galatians 2:20.
8. Luke 9:23.

2

His Way

My Way

Michelle

Culture says: Forge your own way.

God says: My way is the only way.

I have three kids, and while there are many words and skills I've taught them along the way, there's one thing I didn't have to teach them:

Selfishness.

I never taught them to scream "*That's mine!*" when their sibling picks up their beloved toy. Or to yell "*I don't want to!*" when I say it's time to leave the playground. Maybe these phrases sound similar to what you've heard during the toddler years in your home:

Yes, my can. Yes, my do. And of course, the all-time favorite: "*My can do it myself.*"

Immaturity demands its own way, and the premature yearning for independence tends to come as a package deal along with it.

We expect this behavior from toddlers. If you are a parent, you demonstrate your love by affirming the boundaries you've set for their good. But parents can't fully protect their kids forever. Eventually, our kids experience consequences for their disobedience, whether it's a natural consequence (like getting burned by a hot stove they were told not to touch) or a chosen punishment (like losing their car keys for the weekend).

With repetition, they learn. They learn the difference between obedience and disobedience. And though they don't always choose correctly, they learn to make choices, evaluating the risk of disobedience with the security of obedience.

The same natural rebellion exists spiritually: an immaturity on our part that demands its own way along with a foolish desire for independence. Choosing God's way is not our natural inclination.

Choosing *His* way, after all, means abandoning *my* way.

> Trust in the LORD with all your heart,
>   and do not lean on your own understanding.
> In all your ways acknowledge him,
>   and he will make straight your paths.
>
> Proverbs 3:5–6

To call yourself a Christian means you have accepted God as your authority, not your own understanding. Trusting God means I no longer trust myself apart from Him. My way *gladly, fully, and humbly* submits to His way.

Submission Is Not the Problem

I said the word, so we must address it: *submission*. And if that's a prickly word for you, I understand. I used to feel the same way. Culture repeatedly points out that submission is wrong, weak, antiquated, and suppressive.

But that couldn't be further from the clearest example we have of how God designed submission: Jesus. Knowing the cross was before Him, Jesus prayed, "My Father, if it be possible, let this cup pass from me; nevertheless, not as I will, but as you will."[1]

That is submission in action—a strong, spiritual maturity that accepts God's will rather than forcing its own. Jesus' words are courageous, not weak. We don't read that and roll our eyes at Jesus' suppression. We marvel at our Savior's strength.

Trusting God means I no longer trust myself apart from Him. My way gladly, fully, and humbly submits to His way.

In fact, having a problem with submission is evidence that we have submitted to what the world says about submission. So, while I don't expect this to solve all your questions about submission, we can at least resolve to admit that submission isn't the issue. **Sadly, too often we submit to culture far more easily than we submit to God.**

I'm going to be as clear as I can: You cannot submit to Christ and submit to culture. They are not moving in the same direction. And not choosing isn't an option. You must choose, and if you do not actively choose to submit to Christ, your default is to submit to culture.

For example:

- *Gossiping is submitting to culture. Humbly going directly to someone to resolve the problem is submission to God.*
- *Hating your enemies is submitting to culture. Loving your enemies is submission to God.*

1. Matthew 26:39.

- *Exaggerating success is submitting to culture. Not despising small beginnings[2] is submission to God.*
- *Loving money and material possessions is submitting to culture. Loving generosity is submission to God.*
- *Twisting or disregarding Scripture is submitting to culture. Obeying and trusting Scripture—even without full understanding—is submission to God.*

And here's the truth: Culture doesn't just *shift;* culture *drifts.* And you can't drift upstream. Culture drifts into a deeper downward spiral if you are not actively moving against its current.

I'll be honest: I get the appeal. It can often seem like culture has a lot more opportunity to influence us. But please don't be duped. Culture has killer marketing, but it cannot produce what it claims. My way (or your way) isn't unique. In fact, it's just the opposite. It is a wide and broad way—and you're not the only one on it. It "leads to destruction, and those who enter by it are many."[3]

God's way is small and narrow, but it "leads to life."[4] Don't get focused on worldly misconceptions of *narrow* and miss that last part. His way is narrow, not because you're set up for a life of restriction, but because it leads to one destination: *God.* His way is narrow, but the life is full. And the full life that He freely gives requires that we be fully His.

His way *is* the better way.

As You Are Going

I took one Greek class while I was in seminary, and to be clear, I do not consider myself a scholar of the biblical languages. That

2. Zechariah 4:10.
3. Matthew 7:13.
4. Matthew 7:14.

class was one of my hardest academic challenges in my master's degree, but it also provided me one of my greatest spiritual aha moments while studying Matthew 28:18–20.

Known as the Great Commission, these verses hold the final words from Jesus before He ascended into heaven following His resurrection. His last instruction until He comes again:

> And Jesus came and said to them, "All authority in heaven and on earth has been given to me. Go therefore and make disciples of all nations, baptizing them in the name of the Father and of the Son and of the Holy Spirit, teaching them to observe all that I have commanded you. And behold, I am with you always, to the end of the age."
>
> Matthew 28:18–20

Maybe you've previously heard this shared within the context of missions, either a short-term trip or prayers for full-time missionaries, the emphasis being that the command from Jesus is to "go." (Just to be clear, *all nations* does imply that we need to go to the ends of the earth, so it's absolutely appropriate to use this verse in that context.)

But the command *isn't* actually to go. The verb used here, translated *go*, is a present active participle in Greek. A participle is a verb that is functioning as an adjective, and the present active tense indicates a continuous action. So rather than translating this *go* as an action verb, a more accurate translation would be *as you are going.*

So, read it this way: As you are going, **make disciples** of all nations . . .

Jesus' command here is to make disciples. He assumed that we would be going.

As you are going about your daily life, make disciples.

At work . . .

At your child's school activities . . .

At the gym . . .

At church . . .

On vacation . . .

At the grocery store and the mall, in your neighborhood or anywhere between . . .

As you are going . . . *make disciples.*

Making disciples is our main purpose wherever we go. It's not the sidebar, an inconvenience, or an added bonus. It's the point. It's the priority. It's the assumed reason God has us wherever we are. Living this way is pursuing His way before my way.

So what does this look like when it comes to our work?

The Gospel Is Your Job; Your Career Is the Side Hustle

I wish I knew more about Paul's life as a tentmaker. The powerful analogy he made comparing our earthly bodies to tents[5] is proof he knew his craft well. He also took time to connect with others in his trade when he arrived in a new city.[6] But Paul was also clear that the purpose of tentmaking was not to get rich or for his own fulfillment. He worked to support himself and those who traveled with him as they shared the Gospel.[7]

That's what we know. Here's what we don't know for sure, but what I envision:

I don't think Paul pondered how he could be a better tentmaker than his competition (or viewed other tentmakers as competition, for that matter!). I don't think he was jealous over someone else acquiring work he didn't. I can't picture Paul resenting his job as a tentmaker. Given the joy he had in Jesus, I don't think he ever

5. 2 Corinthians 5.
6. Acts 18:1–4.
7. Acts 20:33–35.

dreamed a better job would make him happy or felt tentmaking was beneath him. I doubt that as he worked, he puffed himself up in pride over his incredible tent-making ability.

But I do believe that Paul made high-quality tents so he could continue to get work to provide support for his missionary journeys. I bet he prayed over the people who would purchase the tent and asked God to open doors for him to share the Gospel with his customers. I would love to have eavesdropped on the deep conversations and discipleship I imagine took place as he, Aquila, and Priscilla worked together.

All that we know points to the Gospel being Paul's focus. His career was merely one of the vehicles that made sharing the Gospel possible.

In today's terms, we can understand it like this:

The Gospel is your job. Your career is your side hustle.

Side-Hustle Theology

Let's talk side hustles for a moment. You know what I mean: the woman who has a nine-to-five job and then has another job—the side hustle—she works in every other spare moment she can find.

To be clear, I am not against side hustles any more than I am against your having a traditional job. But have a side hustle only if God calls you to have one—***not because you think you must have one.***

Honestly, those are words I could not have dreamed I would need to type even a few years ago. But we live in a workaholic world, and somehow, women are buying the lie that one job or one business isn't enough, and that a side hustle isn't just for some—it's the only way to prove your legit-ness in the work world.

I could keep the conversation shallow here and we could talk limits of your personal capacity and productivity, but that would neglect this deep truth:

There is often a Gospel cost when we fall into workaholic ways. Being a workaholic leaves us pursuing my way before His way.

Anytime we say yes to something, we say no to something else, even if our no isn't audible. So when we say yes to work and another yes to even more work, what gets our inaudible no?

Often, what falls off our plate or at least moves down on the priority list are community and serving—cornerstones of living the Gospel.

But can't I serve in my work? Absolutely, you can and you should. But we should all have areas of service where we don't receive compensation in return. So rather than making the argument that we serve at work so we don't have to serve elsewhere, we should aim to live a life of service, and realize God is gracious enough to allow serving at work to come with a paycheck.

But I talk about God at work sometimes! Gospel community runs deeper than random conversations about God. Gospel community is the sole purpose of a gathering of believers, where we can pray together, worship, read His Word, and serve one another without the distraction of a secondary task list.

Don't Miss the Spiritual Because of the Secondary

A lot of us miss our spiritual assignments because we're too busy prioritizing secondary conditions.

I want to be able to live this way . . .

I deserve this title . . .

I expect this salary . . .

How quickly we forget that God's preparations rarely look like the path to success the world wants to offer us.

For example:

- *God prepared Joseph to lead Egypt through Joseph's being sold into slavery by his brothers*[8] *and later being wrongfully thrown into prison after he landed in Potiphar's house.*[9]
- *God prepared David to defeat Goliath through David's tending of sheep.*[10]
- *God positioned Esther to save the Jewish people through Esther's journey from orphan to basically winning the real first season of The Bachelor.*[11]

Prioritize the spiritual and trust God for everything else. He's not limited by a particular path He must take for you to end up where He wants you. His way often involves a path you couldn't figure out or find going your own way.

Take my career path, for example. Try to make logical sense of these bullet points:

- *Group fitness instructor/personal trainer to eating disorder*
- *Eating disorder to call to ministry*
- *Call to ministry to pharmaceutical sales*
- *Pharmaceutical sales to severance package*
- *Severance package to seminary*
- *Seminary to church position*
- *Church position to network marketing*
- *Network marketing to online retail*
- *Online retail to She Works HIS Way*

No business consultant would ever recommend or plan the path I took. But looking back, I can see God's purpose behind every step . . . *including* my missteps.

8. Genesis 37:18–36.
9. Genesis 39:19–21.
10. 1 Samuel 17:34–37.
11. Esther 2.

For example, take my brief pit stop in pharmaceutical sales that was also semi running from my call to ministry: Nothing could have better prepared me for network marketing rejection than learning to sell to doctors.

And speaking of network marketing, who gets a theology degree to do *that*? Well, the woman who still had a lot she needed God to show her through her hands-on learning style, and who needed to understand the struggle of faith, family, and work before she could minister effectively to women like her. Plus, God used part of the earnings of that business to serve as the investment for She Works HIS Way.

It doesn't have to look right, feel right, or be exactly what you thought it would be for you to be in the center of God's will for your life. But we can certainly miss God's will if we're too busy waiting on what's next to serve where He has us right now.

Understanding God's calling on our life is often as simple as asking ourselves *Where does God have me?* instead of asking *How does God want to use me?*

Wherever God has you right now, He has plans to use you there. It's through the seemingly small steps of obedience that He positions us and significantly shapes us for the future. God won't waste anywhere He takes you. What human logic sees as a detour is often God working out the details. Your my-way path may make sense, but His way leads somewhere beyond your imagination and your ask.[12]

Change Bosses

Only when we try to make God's work about ourselves do we reach for ways to highlight our own importance. There's no issue when His way and my way align, but what about when

12. Ephesians 3:20.

they don't? Who wins? Ultimately, those moments are the ones that reveal who you believe is actually in charge—you or God.

The "be your own boss" mantra is strong. With #girlboss, #bossbabe, #ladyboss, and dozens of others, it's hard to be a working woman without encountering these movements. Not even ministry is exempt. The #girlpreacher movement is cut from the same cloth as #girlboss. (Culture takes a little longer to reach the church, but eventually it finds its way in.) These culture-driven trends lend themselves quickly to selfishness. And the mindsets that accompany them cannot complement the Christian life; they only compete with it. God's callings are always rooted in the work—not numbers, titles, or any other earthly measurements. Peter warns that our fleshly passions "wage war against your soul."[13]

Fifteen years ago, God called me to dedicate my life to proclaiming His Word. So, from volunteering in my local church to dinner tables with family and friends, posting on social media, bedtime routines with my kids, building a network marketing business, one-on-one conversations, and countless other avenues across ministry *and* secular settings, I've never once found myself in a situation where preaching wasn't possible.

So any time or energy I would spend fighting to be known as a #girlpreacher would steal from *actually* preaching. Elevating myself steals from the work. That's what prioritizing my way does. It makes it about what you want instead of what is *really* needed.

I don't say this boastfully, but because I know how easily my flesh could draw me in to be the ringleader of every female empowerment movement. So whether you need to remind yourself that you are not the boss of your life or that you answer to a Boss much higher than yourself or your supervisor at work, as Christ-followers we have one Boss:

13. 1 Peter 2:11.

> Whatever you do, work heartily, as for the Lord and not for men, knowing that from the Lord you will receive the inheritance as your reward. You are serving the Lord Christ.
>
> Colossians 3:23–24

This is not our home, and our Boss is in heaven. Whatever we're doing, we are to be serving Christ.

Whatever You Do

Work that is done for Christ, then, cannot ever be defined by the task, but by our Boss.

Elisabeth Elliot put it this way: "There is no such thing as Christian work. That is, there is no work in the world, which is, in and of itself, Christian. Christian work is any kind of work, from cleaning a sewer to preaching a sermon, that is done by a Christian and offered to God."[1]

Let's rewrite the script. Christian work isn't defined by the task you do, but by your decision to do the work and offer it to God.

By the way, part of the reason this is so hard to put into practice is because this is the polar opposite of the world's advice that you'll finally be fulfilled at work when you figure out how to get paid for your passion (which will be quickly followed by figuring out how to get paid more for your passion).

Please let me caution you against believing that lie. No job can truly satisfy anyone, and that is *especially true for you as a Christ-follower* because you have the Holy Spirit inside of you, who loves you too much to be silent when you seek satisfaction outside of God.

But let's zoom out wider. "Whatever you do" applies to just that: *whatever you do*. That means your career is included in this instruction, but these words are not limited to your job.

As a believer, your work ethic is determined by your energy in God's overall mission of making disciples, the assignments He's given you at home and in your relationships, and finally, yes, in your career . . . in that order.

Have you allowed yourself to minimize your work ethic to your energy in your career? At one point, I did. And so did my friend Anna.

Anna's Story

At first, Anna reminded me of the younger me: always striving but never satisfied. To her credit, she accomplished most of the goals she set out to achieve, but despite feeling that "*This is it!*" each time she set out on the next thing, the result was always the same: Hitting the goal was never enough, and she was always left wanting more.

But one year, everything changed. Instead of setting dozens of goals when a new year rolled around, Anna set only one: to read the entire Bible. She had been attending church and even Bible studies since she was a child, but she had never really dug into God's Word on her own consistently.

The change in her wasn't immediate, but every time we talked, small changes were evident. There was a difference in the way she carried herself, the way she spoke and interacted with others. And it wasn't that she stopped setting goals, but after a few months, I could tell that *she had stopped setting her mind on goals, and she set her mind on things above.*[14]

It was such a joy to watch Anna fall deeper and deeper in love with Jesus. She shared through early morning texts as she uncovered a new truth or simply got excited about what she was learning. God was at work in her life, and as a natural

14. Colossians 3:2.

extension, He was also working through her to minister to others.

In her own words: "To most who knew me, my life might not have looked that different, but I knew the drastic difference that was happening. After spending my adult life up to that point striving to do what God wanted, largely in my own power, I was becoming a surrendered woman who desired only what He wanted for me."[2]

In January of the following year, Anna got a phone call from the company she had nearly idolized and wanted to work for throughout most of her career. I *was* excited for her, but I also instantly felt my spiritual-sister protective mode kick in. If there was an opportunity that could convince her to spiral into old habits, this was the one.

But I was instantly comforted by what she said next:

> It's the weirdest thing. If this had happened a decade ago, I would be in straight-up campaign mode right now. "Get hired" would be the only option available in my mind. Don't get me wrong. I'm excited, and I'm grateful, but I'm also cautious—a word I have rarely used in my life. If this opportunity isn't from God, then I don't want it. Please pray I will be able to discern if this is from Him or not, that I will learn something one way or the other, and that I will have the courage to walk away if this isn't God's timing or God's plan for me.[3]

(Read that one more time. That text is a sermon in itself!)

So Anna went to the meeting. She loved every person she met. The company culture was incredible. Everything she'd thought for the last decade was true. This would be an incredible place to work, and it would open doors for her to help a lot of people.

Career wise, it was a no-brainer. Financially, it was by far the responsible choice. And as far as opportunities and networking, this partnership would open doors she had dreamed of for years. Logically, it was the smartest next step.

But spiritually, she felt like she would be taking a step back, and she couldn't shake the discernment of the Holy Spirit—it wasn't where God was directing her steps.[15] Choosing His way, she walked away from something almost anyone in her position would have deemed the opportunity of a lifetime.

But here's the really amazing part: She walked away *joyfully* not reluctantly, completely free of FOMO (fear of missing out), because God had not only answered her prayer, but He filled her with His peace that surpasses understanding.[16] She didn't have to know what His way would entail to be confident His way was best.

"Yes," Anna wrote, "that position would have elevated me to the next level in my career, for sure, but it would have also meant taking steps away from what God has called me to do, and that's just not an option anymore. So, I'm more excited than ever to follow Him! I would have never dreamed anything could be better than what I walked away from—but I'm confident His plans are always better than mine, and I am here for it."[4]

Anna's story best illustrates the difference between striving and surrender:

Striving says, "I've got this." Surrender says, "God's got me."

Surrendered Effort

Like submission, biblical surrender is often misunderstood. A life of surrender is not absent of action; the surrendered person just doesn't plow ahead without the Lord.

15. Proverbs 16:9.
16. Philippians 4:7.

Perhaps the best example of this is found in Exodus. You've probably seen a beautiful image of Exodus 14:14 on your Instagram feed before:

"The Lord will fight for you, and you have only to be silent."

But have you ever read the verses that follow?

> The Lord said to Moses, "Why do you cry to me? Tell the people of Israel to go forward. Lift up your staff, and stretch out your hand over the sea and divide it, that the people of Israel may go through the sea on dry ground."
>
> vv. 15–16

Was God rebuking Moses for praying? Absolutely not. Prayer is an important part of kingdom work, but we shouldn't use prayer as an excuse for spiritual procrastination. There is a time to pray, and there is a time to act. Biblical surrender *gets* still[17] but doesn't *stay* still.

The ebb and flow of prayer and action is the rhythm of the Christian life—which I've come to call "surrendered effort," adapted from these words from D. A. Carson:

> Apart from **grace-driven effort,** people do not gravitate toward godliness, prayer, obedience to Scripture, faith, and delight in the Lord. We drift toward compromise and call it tolerance; we drift toward disobedience and call it freedom; we drift toward superstition and call it faith. We cherish the indiscipline of lost self-control and call it relaxation; we slouch toward prayerlessness and delude ourselves into thinking we have escaped legalism; we slide toward godlessness and convince ourselves we have been liberated.[5]

17. Psalm 46:10.

Surrendered effort is intentional movement in God's direction. Otherwise, we only drift in one direction, even if we feel like we're striving with all of our strength—which is precisely the problem:

Striving is limited by your strength, while surrender relies on God's strength.

Here's a visual showing the difference between being stuck in the striving cycle vs. living in the freedom of surrendered effort:

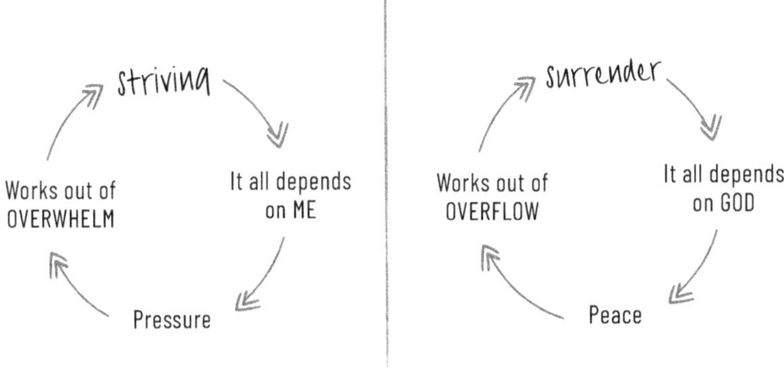

When you're *striving*, you bear the load as though it all depends on you. It's an immense pressure you were not designed to bear, but despite your exhaustion, despite being overwhelmed, you press on anyway, determined that there's nothing you won't do to make it happen; the work will be worth it eventually . . . assuming you end up getting what you want.

But when you *surrender*, you realize that results are in God's hands. Because of His past faithfulness, you have peace in God's presence alone. In step with the Spirit,[18] you allow God to continue to work in you, which gives Him room to work through

18. Galatians 5:25.

you. And even if God chooses an outcome you never would have chosen, you fully trust that He's working for His glory[19] and your good.[20]

Take Back Ambition

Surrendered effort also does not mean that you live a life void of ambition. Honestly, it grieves me to think about ambition belonging to the world. Please don't stop being ambitious. The opposite of selfish ambition is not spiritual laziness but channeling your ambition for the kingdom—not for yourself.

Several times throughout the New Testament, our faith is compared to running a race. One of my favorites is Hebrews 12:1–2:

> Therefore, since we are surrounded by so great a cloud of witnesses, let us also lay aside every weight, and sin which clings so closely, and let us run with endurance the race that is set before us, looking to Jesus, the founder and perfecter of our faith, who for the joy that was set before him endured the cross, despising the shame, and is seated at the right hand of the throne of God.

John Piper shared from a sermon he heard on this text that had impacted him as a teen, urging believers not to ask the minimum question, "Is this a sin?" But to ask the maximum question, "Does it help me run?"[6]

Examine the scope of your work—from God's mission to your home to your career—and evaluate what's on your plate:

Looking to Jesus, what helps you run? Prioritize those things.

19. Isaiah 42:8.
20. Romans 8:28.

And looking to Jesus, what's slowing you down? Lay them down.

Selfish ambition is often merely a matter of doing *more*, but kingdom ambition is a matter of doing *right*.

It's really that simple. My way may get things done, but His way *does what matters*.

A Prayer to Put His Way Before My Way

Father, forgive me when rebellion and immaturity
Demand my own way and seek independence from
You.
Reveal to me when I am leaning on my own
understanding,
Rather than trusting You with all my heart.[21]

End my natural concession to culture,
And strengthen my submission to You.
God, I fully and joyfully accept Your will for my life,
And I commit to stop forcing my own.

God, Your ways and understanding are infinitely above
my own,[22]
So help me go Your way, even when I can't comprehend
it.
Erase the allure of being in control and in charge,
Be the Boss over every area of my life.

Mark my life with surrendered effort.
I no longer want to be a woman who simply gets things
done,
But I want to be a woman who does what matters,
Because I solely do what matters to You.

God, there's no job or task that can satisfy me.
Keep me running to Your presence,
The only place where satisfaction is found.
Replace all of my desires for what's next
With vision for Your mission where You have me now.

21. Proverbs 3:5.
22. Isaiah 55:8–9.

Help me stop compartmentalizing my work ethic to my job,
And to start treating every moment with kingdom potential.
As I go, open doors for me to make disciples.
Use every inch of my influence for Your kingdom.
The Gospel can no longer be my side hustle, Lord,
But it must be the mission that my every effort flows from.

Put my confidence in Christ alone,
And make everything I do an offering to You.
Lord, "Your kingdom come" means my kingdom must go.[23]
Steady my steps on holy ground.

Amen.

23. Matthew 6:10.

3

Lose Myself

Find Myself

Somer

Some of us love to listen to a good story, and some of us love to tell them—but either way, we're a people who love a gripping tale. So it makes sense that many of the most lucrative industries are those that have something to do with storytelling—cinema, literature, art, music, etc. These industries are most successful when they tell really good stories.

But why do we love stories so much?

- *Good stories give our brain a place to travel so it makes for a nice escape from our daily grind.*
- *They remind us that the good guys usually win in the end, which makes us feel good (or at least better!) about humanity.*

- *Sometimes, we immediately relate to one of the characters, which makes us instantly feel understood and kind of special.*

But pretty much always, whether or not we love a story line centers around the way the story makes us feel.

So let's talk about the greatest story ever told: the Bible. It's this beautiful story about God constantly pursuing His people—you and me. At the same time, it's also a tragic story about how we turn away from Him over and over again.

Unlike the movies, Scripture does not paint a pretty picture of us and our sin. Our rebellion is not cute. Our independence is not noble. And our stubbornness is called out for exactly what it is—selfishness.

I'll be honest, this is why I get a bit frustrated when we tell women to "just read your Bible" but forget to prepare them for the discomfort as well as the wrestling they are likely to encounter.

We head to our cozy corner with our warm cup of coffee expecting Jesus to meet us with sweet words and a gentle hug. And some days, that's exactly what He does.

But other days? He may not.

Scripture should be the means we use to get to know the God who created us in the most intimate of ways. In learning about Him, we will no doubt learn more about ourselves . . . *but it won't always be the things we want to know.*

So there we have it, the answer to why it's not always easy to read our Bibles consistently:

It's not that we don't have the right reading plan or the perfect journaling Bible, but that we don't love the way what we're reading forces us to examine our own hearts.

And because, although the Bible was written for us, its primary goal is not to help us find ourselves but to move us to lose ourselves—and that's just not as fun sometimes.

The truth of the matter is, we don't need extra motivation to make ourselves *feel good*. We need extra motivation to make ourselves *be holy*.

And listen, reading and studying the Bible, the story of our redemption, is the best way to get and stay motivated toward holiness.

Now let me be clear, for those of you who have heard women say that they "crave God's Word," you can believe that. Jesus said, "Blessed are those who hunger and thirst for righteousness, for they will be filled."[1]

I know I crave His Word in a real way. Sometimes, in moments of anxiousness, I find myself reaching for the Bible just to hold it. His Word truly is living and active.[2]

But it hasn't always been like this for me.

There was a time in my life I could go about my day without spending time in my Bible, believing my lack of being in the Word didn't affect me. But once I started allowing God's Word to change me, I was made aware of the very real ways my lack of being in God's Word affected my thoughts, behaviors, and attitude, as well as my relationships and interactions with others.

So please be encouraged. If you're struggling to consistently read God's Word, it's completely possible for you to move from where you are to a place where His Word becomes as critical to your daily routine as other basic needs.

But craving time with the Lord in the same way you need food or water will require you to push through some ugly parts. The parts that remind you of who you are without God.

The only way to truly find yourself is to lose yourself in God and His Word.

1. Matthew 5:6 CSB.
2. Hebrews 4:12.

Dying to Find Ourselves

As a Bible-believing Christian woman, I have heard the identity sermon given at nearly every women's conference and retreat that I've attended. It's an important truth for us to comprehend, so I understand the constant reminder to find our identity in Christ alone.[3]

But why does it rarely stick? Why is it so easy to forget that we are *daughters of the King*?[4] That seems like a pretty big deal, right?

I think it's because we skip Step 1:

> And he [Jesus] said to all, "If anyone would come after me, let him deny himself and take up his cross daily and follow me."
>
> Luke 9:23

We're great at claiming the title *daughter of the King*, but we're not so great with the dying to self we need to do before we can *live* the title. And no matter how many times we recommit to finding this new identity, without dying to ourselves first we will never be prepared to live in this identity.

Paul may not have been the most popular women's retreat speaker (although if it were possible, he would probably be our top choice for our SWHW annual Narrow Conference). But Paul explains identity in one of the most powerful ways in his letter to the church in Galatia:

> I have been crucified with Christ. It is no longer I who live, but Christ who lives in me. And the life I now live in the flesh I live by faith in the Son of God, who loved me and gave himself for me.
>
> Galatians 2:19–20

3. Colossians 3:3.
4. Galatians 3:26; John 1:12; Ephesians 1:5; 1 Peter 2:9.

Don't miss this: It's not so much about *finding* our identity in Christ as it is about our *awareness* of our identity in Christ. Once we stop living and Christ takes over, it is impossible to find our identity in anything but Him. When we die to self, our former identities—whether in our looks, talent, career, or whatever—they die too.

Addicted to Affirmation

I have never heard people talk about affirmation as much as I have in recent years. It seems to be a requirement for healthy relationships at home and at work. There's nothing wrong with celebrating each other. In fact, as believers, we're called to encourage and edify one another.[5] But as can anything, affirmation can become an addiction.

Not a minor addiction, mind you, but an addiction that will eventually lead you to value the voices of people over the voice of God. And it happens more easily than we'd like to think.

Because often, as soon as our Creator begins to reveal anything about you that isn't all unicorns and rainbows, the temptation will be to quiet His voice and subscribe to the voices that we'd rather hear! Those that say something more like "I am woman, hear me roar."

Paul actually warned Timothy about this in the last letter he wrote before he died: "For the time will come when people will not put up with sound doctrine. Instead, to suit their own desires, they will gather around them a great number of teachers to say what their itching ears want to hear."[6]

Please don't let itching ears cause you to miss the godly wisdom that is vital to your spiritual life.

5. 1 Thessalonians 5:11; Hebrews 10:24–25; Ecclesiastes 4:9–12.
6. 2 Timothy 4:3 NIV.

Something I've learned through the years is that most of the time, our addiction to affirmation is just a symptom of discontentment with ourselves. Not only that, but this discontentment is always, *always*, a result of not seeing ourselves as God's creation.

I knew an artist who painted a gorgeous but very personal piece of art. He was invited to participate in a show at a local gallery, and despite some hesitancy, he said yes. He proudly hung his artwork on the wall and stepped to the side to admire it.

But later that evening, a pseudo-intellectual art critic began to tell him all that he could have done to make the painting more attractive. My friend looked at him and said, "Thank you for your feedback, but this piece was made for my pleasure, and to my eyes, it's perfect."

God created you for His pleasure, for His glory, and for His purpose. You can search as long as you want to find yourself, but you will never know yourself like your heavenly Father knows you. Even the hairs on your head are numbered (including the gray ones that seem to be coming in at warp speed like mine, and the brown ones that are in desperate need of a little bleach like Michelle's. He knows them all!).[7]

Thinking that we can find ourselves apart from finding our Maker is terribly misguided. The very essence of who we are was knit together by Him. Let's take a second to slow down and notice the word picture used in Scripture to explain how we came to be.

"For you formed my inward parts; you knitted me together in my mother's womb" (Psalm 139:13).

"Knitted me together"—what a mind-blowing description! Especially considering that God could have totally just abracadabraed us into existence. But instead, He personally created us

7. Luke 12:7.

as unique individuals made with all the gifts, strengths, weaknesses, abilities, disabilities, and everything else in between, so that we would be equipped to fulfill our purpose for His glory.

When you need affirmation from anyone outside of Him, the only reason is because you have forgotten that His eyes are the only eyes that matter.[8] An outsider's opinion should never carry more weight than the truth that you are your Creator's very good idea and are made in His image.[9] But when you forget who you really are, affirmation from others is the first thing you're likely to look for.

Thinking that we can find ourselves apart from finding our Maker is terribly misguided.

Knowing and seeing God for who He is is the *only* way we will ever find ourselves and see ourselves as He sees us.

And that matters because **the way God sees you is who you really are.**

Wants + Feelings + Passion = Trouble

The "find myself" movement has basically become a rite of passage. It's been around for a very long time, and interestingly enough, it's largely a female trend.

In a simple Google search one day, I typed in: "*Why do I need to find myself?*"

There were hundreds of pages worth of results, but I didn't have to scroll far to read the overall consensus on this question. Over and over, I read that the reason you need to find yourself is because knowing who you are will help you *know* what you want, and then *get* what you want.

8. Psalm 45:11.
9. Genesis 1:26–31.

Can you hear how narcissistic that sounds? Know who you are so you can know what you want and get what you want. Yet, the practice of women spending time on this journey is praised—even within the Christian community.

Here's a little comparison chart that might help us with some self-evaluation. Which column best represents the questions your mind dwells on?

Questions to Find Yourself	**Questions to Lose Yourself**
1. What makes me feel happy?	1. What makes me joyful?
2. What makes me feel popular?	2. What makes me loved?
3. What makes me feel successful?	3. What makes me obedient?
4. What makes me feel powerful?	4. Where does my power come from?
5. What makes me comfortable?	5. What makes me purposeful?
6. What makes me feel noticed?	6. How do I know I matter?
7. What do I want?	7. Where does my treasure lie?

Notice the difference in the questions we ask when we're more concerned with losing ourselves than finding ourselves. And find the word that you see over and over in the left column but is missing from the right column: *feel*.

This will not be the first Christian book to remind you that following your feelings will get you into all sorts of trouble. But refusing to follow your feelings is a very unpopular notion.

My daughters are eighteen and twenty, and the world is already preaching to them:

Do what makes you happy!

Follow your dreams.

Decide what you want and go after it!

Maybe you've been bombarded by those messages too.

Rhinestone Halter Tops

About fifteen years ago, every morning I would kiss my girls goodbye, walk out to get in my mom SUV (that was always running on fumes because getting gas would make me late), and head to work in rush-hour traffic in Fort Worth, Texas. My husband, Kent, was full-time in seminary and working at UPS loading boxes onto trucks on the overnight shift. My girls were in preschool and kindergarten, arguably the cutest ages children can be, and I was running a high-end boutique where I spent fifty-plus hours a week.

I didn't hate my job, but I very rarely *felt* like going to work. I especially dreaded the drive to work. Most of my commute was spent muttering bitter words under my breath. I knew better than to say them to God (as if He didn't already know), but I also couldn't keep them in.

I started working when I was fifteen, and I loved work *immediately*. I loved the feeling of independence, the feeling of making a difference, and especially the feeling of payday. But motherhood changed my desires. It made me want to be home with my babies.

I wanted to learn how to cook, to spend my days decluttering and decorating our tiny apartment. I wanted to have picnics in the park and attend story time at the library. I wanted to work out and take care of myself.

And in my mind, every single thing that I felt that I desired (and maybe even deserved), would only be possible if I could quit my job. But I was the breadwinner at that time, so it just wasn't a possibility. That was a really hard season.

I also need to let you know that my walk with the Lord was not where it needed to be. Not even close. Oh, the pain I could have saved myself if I had been chasing Him as hard as I was fighting Him!

Every time I talk to a woman who says, "But Somer, this is not what I want to do. It's not my passion. What I *feel* like I want to do is . . ." I can go back to how I felt in those days instantly. I totally understand! And in those conversations, I tell her what I wish I could go back and tell myself:

Your feelings are the voice your flesh uses to communicate to you. And let me tell you right now, your flesh doesn't have anything good to say.

Selling rhinestone halter tops to cowboys' wives *was not* my passion, but it was my assignment. And more than that, it was God's provision for our lives.

Somehow, we have made ourselves believe that if we don't feel like doing it, we probably shouldn't have to do it.

My issue with my work was that I was so focused inward (on finding myself, my way, my preference) I missed everything happening outwardly, and there was so much!

Someday, if you and I have a chance to go get coffee, I will tell you about all God did in my life during that time to draw me closer to Him. Not to mention all the stories of people I had the honor of introducing to Jesus while I was just doing my job. Selling rhinestone halter tops.

We have to stop using our feelings as a compass when we have something so much better. An actual Guide who goes before you,[10] holding your hand,[11] and directing your every step.[12]

10. Deuteronomy 31:8.
11. Isaiah 41:13.
12. Proverbs 16:9.

Finding ourselves will lead us to listen to our feelings.
Losing ourselves will lead us to God.

Working Woman Culture

Remember the Garden of Eden? Adam was tasked with taking care of it. Do you ever think about the fact that the first job given to man was gardening?

God didn't allow Adam time to find himself and discover his passions. And Adam wasn't concerned with choosing a career path that would fulfill him because God was the One who did that.

We have it so twisted!

Is it okay to love your work? Absolutely!

Is it okay if you don't love your work? Absolutely!

The point is that our contentment comes from the One who created us—not from the work we create.

I have some pretty amazing working woman friends I depend on when I need to talk to someone who just "gets it." But what the Instagram feed won't tell you about working women is that not all of us are obsessed with our careers. Some of us work because God has asked us to or because we have a gift or a skill that is desperately needed.

For example, here are a few of the jobs held by some of the real women in my life:

- *one of the top-producing pharmaceutical reps in her territory*
- *CEO of a design firm*
- *nurse practitioner who specializes in neurological critical care and saves lives every day (my sister—so I can brag!)*
- *VP of operations for a large company in the Northeast*
- *director of Women's Ministry in her church.*

What do all of these women have in common? They're trained, educated, qualified, and they work hard. But guess what else: Not one defines herself by her job title. How do I know that? Because I knew some of them for months before I ever learned what they did for work.

But here's what these women do not have in common with the *working woman culture* of today: They understand that their work is the place that God has called them to and is not necessarily the place their passion has taken them. Subsequently, they don't depend on their career for contentment, and they are aware that although there may be more comfort and freedom in a side hustle, comfort and freedom are not the point or the purpose of their lives.

Maybe you're like my friends. You're not necessarily discontent with your day job, but you feel pressured to take on a side hustle or find something you're more passionate about. Please don't give in to the pressure. Those are not reasons to quit. Only God can give quitting orders, so listen to Him and stay where you're called. The world desperately needs Christian women in *all* fields. Your co-workers need to be pointed to Jesus! Your clients/students/patients need to be loved like Jesus loves! You are vital to His mission right where you are.

If Adam was cool with gardening, we can be cool with our less flashy assignments too.

The Study of Us

Raise your hand if you've ever taken a personality test. Okay, you can put it down. (If you actually raised your hand, please know that I am laughing at the thought of it and I love you! Also, if you've ever wondered if you're really a rule follower, wonder no more.)

Okay, before you think I'm going to get judgy—I've taken most of the tests that are out there and learned a lot. So first things first, learning about yourself isn't always a bad idea, but it's also not a new idea. This deep desire to self-analyze goes way back to early Greeks, like Plato, who explored approaches to psychometric measurements.

Finding ourselves will lead us to listen to our feelings. Losing ourselves will lead us to God.

So as much as we may see it as trendy to introduce yourself with a number rather than a name (Enneagram lovers, I'm talking to us), the idea behind this trend has been around forever. But why?

Because humans very much need something to study and worship.

We are born with an innate need to find God and to worship Him. It's a need we're acutely aware of, and many spend their entire lives trying to satisfy that desire with other things. On the most basic level, the difference between believers and nonbelievers is that nonbelievers have given in to their stubborn nature and decided to put their faith and trust in something else, while believers put their faith and trust in God.

You see, we will put our faith and trust in something. Sometimes it's religion, sometimes relationships, sometimes leaders or politics.

But most of the time, we simply put our faith in ourselves. This is why personality tests and any self-focused work can be a slippery slope. Because it's really hard to lose yourself when your greatest focus *is* yourself.

Learning about yourself is not a bad idea. But an obsession with the study of yourself, or the tools that bring us those answers, might be.

So take all the tests, learn all the things, and buy all the T-shirts. But understand that if this information is not used for the glory of God and the good of others, you've made it about you.

And I'd be remiss not to remind you that if you really want to understand yourself, you do have access to the One who wired you.

Need to know the ins and outs of a house? Ask the builder.

Need a comprehensive understanding of software? Ask the developer.

Need to know the meaning of a painting? Ask the artist.

Don't neglect the One who knows your words before you speak them and is familiar with all your ways[13] for some popular test that makes you feel better about your issues. God's got the answers you really need.

And more than that, God's got you!

So let go of finding yourself and get completely and totally lost in Him. Like a tiny broken piece of a seashell that has made its way to the shore but gets swept up by the next wave and dumped back into the depths of the magnificent ocean.

Get *that* kind of lost.

13. Psalm 139:1–4.

A Prayer to Lose Myself in a Find-Myself World

Father, I come before You
With eyes that are only on You.
In the moments when my eyes wander back toward me,
Fix my eyes back on You, the Pioneer and Perfecter of my faith.[14]

Forgive me for my sins of self-reliance, self-obsession, self-empowerment, and self-idolization.
Open my eyes to see myself only as You see me.
Rid me of my fleshly fascination with how the world sees me.

When I feel confused about who I am,
help me to rest assured in Who You are.
"It is no longer I who live, but Christ who lives in me.
And the life I now live in the flesh I live by faith."[15]

When I feel sure of who I am without You,
Convict me quickly to sprint into Your presence.
Reveal the outside influences in my life that have fed me and led me to believe
I can fulfill my purpose without You.

And when I am sure of Who I am because I am Your daughter,
Let the overwhelming joy of those moments overflow
So that others may see Your glory
And experience Your goodness through me.

14. Hebrews 12:2 CSB.
15. Galatians 2:20.

And God, please multiply those days
So those are the days my life is marked by.

Father, my heart longs to know You wholly and
completely.
To know and comprehend all of Your ways.
But until the day I am made whole in Your presence,
I pray for faith that is more powerful than proof.

Faith that confidently and boldly walks in my purpose.
Faith that reminds me Who You are when my flesh
begins to doubt.
Faith that moves me to do all that You've called me to
do.
Faith that I get lost in.
Faith where You alone are found.

Father, help me to lose myself in You so greatly
That I am unable to find myself without You ever
again.

Amen.

4

Know God

Be Known

Michelle

Culture says: To be known is to be powerful.

God says: Know Me and experience My power.

God created us to know Him and to worship Him, and refers to us as "the people I formed for myself that they may proclaim my praise" (Isaiah 43:21 NIV). So everyone worships. Not everyone worships God, but we all worship something.

Some choose to worship money, pleasure, success, or their career, which are easier to identify as problematic. But others worship "good" things, like the well-meaning mom who worships her kids, or the pastor who worships his church and ministry.

Want to know the one thing all good things have in common? No matter how good, all good things fall short of being God.

And not only is God the only One worthy of our worship, but God is the only One who can withstand being worshiped.

The child who is worshiped by his parents, for example, will not be able to bear the weight of being the source of their parents' identity forever. The stock market? It can crash. Jobs can be lost. Careers can crumble. Heroes can fail.

Only God can be God.

So when we talk about knowing God, I don't want us to confuse knowing God with knowing about God, because there really is a difference. Our worship—rather than how much theological knowledge we have or even how much Scripture we can recall—is really the best indicator of how deeply we know God.

And worship goes far beyond a music genre. I love the definition of worship given by my pastor, Bruce Frank, who says, "Worship is my head, heart, and hands responding to who God is and what God has done."

If you want to know what you worship, ask yourself: *What are my head, heart, and hands responding to most often?*

Or this question: **What do I make bigger in my life?** Because we make bigger what we worship.

Really reflect on your deepest desire or your greatest struggle. Do your answers to those two questions lead back to God and His purposes, or do they have more to do with you and your own desires?

Because the truth is, when the biggest thing in your life isn't wrapped up in God and His agenda, that reveals an even bigger problem than the one you may think you have:

God needs to be bigger in your life.

When God is not paramount, we run the risk of knowing about Him, but not actually knowing Him. Because it's only when God is the biggest part of our lives that less important things can matter less. And it's only when He is the sole object of our worship that we accurately understand who God is.

And if we don't know who God is, we'll end up with a skewed view of who we are.

So what's the worst culprit that keeps us from knowing God? Our pride.

Pride exists in many forms and many arenas, but in the work world, one of the biggest spiritual obstacles we face is that we are constantly being told that in order for us and our work to matter, we must be known.

Social media really became a thing when I was in college, so I'm part of that middle generation—old enough to easily remember life without it, but young enough to have been part of the first target audience. And between reality TV, TikTok, YouTube, Instagram stories, and Facebook Live, being known is a much greater possibility for all of us than ever before.

Platforms aren't just established on stages anymore, and you don't really have to earn the right to have one. With the click of a button, your thoughts and ideas are out there, never to be fully erased, and there's really no progression from smaller stages to the larger ones. Everyone starts with the entire world as their potential reach.

And while an actual stage used to be available a few times a week at most, even for the most sought-after communicators, our phones allow each of us the opportunity to be at center stage every day. And while we used to have adequate time to prepare and recover before and after taking the stage, we have become so digitally dependent as a whole that most of us take our stage with us to the bathroom, the dinner table, the stoplight while driving, etc. So most of our digital interaction is done mindlessly, as opposed to prayerfully and intentionally.

Really let this sink in: Practically every second of your day provides you with the opportunity to elevate yourself more easily than ever before. We can't be passive about dealing with pride; we must intentionally fight against it. Otherwise, our pride will fight against our kingdom impact.

Sharing the Stage

I've already admitted to you that I have battled being an approval junkie my entire life. From home videos when I was a toddler to extracurricular activities I chose in school, it's not hard to see: I loved an audience and I loved applause.

I wish I could tell you that before I began ministry, my motives had changed, but they really hadn't. For longer than I'd like to admit, I allowed myself to feel special because, in a room full of people, I was the one who got the microphone. I did love God; I wanted to teach what His Word says and I wanted God to get the glory. But I still wanted some of the credit.

Basically, I wanted to share the stage. It never gets easier to admit that. I cringe at those memories. There's nothing godly about trying to share a stage with Jesus.

Maybe you need to hear the lessons I had to learn over the years as He pruned me:

It's not possible for your work to be all about Him if part of you still desires for some of it to be a little about you.

But because it's easier than ever to fall into the pattern of the world that is daily seeking affirmation and approval, we must be more intentional than ever to stop any unnecessary focus on us. And when we allow special treatment because of our spiritual gifts or the positions we hold, that steals focus and attention away from where it belongs: on Jesus.

I believe God still uses servants today to get His message out, and sometimes that will include large audiences. But if a large audience becomes the goal, the real goal is missed.

In Kingdom work, the world coming to know God is the goal, not you or me being made known to the world.

Let's dig into God's Word for an example of someone who did this right.

Unique to Be Obedient (Not to Gain Attention)

Admit it: You'd be curious to hear what a preacher had to say if he walked into your church looking like he came straight out of the wilderness. Well, that's how the people of his day felt about John the Baptist.

From what he wore to what he ate to the words he used, John was drastically different from the other religious leaders. And his way of life wasn't the only thing different about John. His message was different too.

In Kingdom work, the world coming to know God is the goal, not you or me being made known to the world.

John basically had one sermon: Over and over again, he called the crowds to repentance for their sins, and he promised them that the Messiah was coming after him. But here's the catch:

Nothing about the way he lived was an attempt to impress anyone or a manipulative strategy. The point of his uniqueness was obedience, not attention. John was simply following the call on his life that an angel had revealed to his father, Zechariah (Luke 1:11–17) before he was born.

And although his message wasn't a comfortable one, large crowds were drawn to him, demanding over and over again to know who he was (John 1:19–23). The crowds following John continued to grow, and he baptized many daily as they chose to repent of their sins.

But John never wavered in his identity or his message: His mission wasn't to be the one known but to prepare people to know Jesus when His ministry began. And as soon as Jesus came on the scene, that's exactly what John did.

John's Ultimate Goal: Get Unfollowed

The day after the crowds questioned John about who he was, John saw Jesus walking toward him and declared, "Behold, the Lamb of God, who takes away the sin of the world!"[1]

The day after that, John was standing in the same place with two of his disciples and Jesus walked by again, and John said, "Behold, the Lamb of God!" But this time, the story doesn't stop there. Two of John's disciples listened to his words, and they began following Jesus themselves.[2]

Don't miss what happened here: They stopped following John so they could follow Jesus.

From there, Jesus' public ministry took off. He began choosing disciples of His own, performed His first public miracle at a wedding, turning water into wine, and even revealed God's plan to save the world through Him to a Jewish leader.[3]

John continued to preach repentance and to point others to Jesus. But some of those following him still didn't get it. John's disciples came to him, concerned, and said, "Rabbi, he who was with you across the Jordan, to whom you bore witness—look, he is baptizing, and all are going to him."[4]

John's disciples were worried that John's ministry was dwindling, when John knew that his crowd's shifting to Jesus was proof his ministry had been effective.

Read John's next words, and let's take them to heart:

> John answered, "A person cannot receive even one thing unless it is given him from heaven. You yourselves bear me witness, that I said, 'I am not the Christ, but I have been sent before him.' The one who has the bride is the bridegroom. The friend

1. John 1:29.
2. John 1:35–37.
3. John 1:35–3:21.
4. John 3:26.

> of the bridegroom, who stands and hears him, rejoices greatly at the bridegroom's voice. Therefore this joy of mine is now complete. He must increase, but I must decrease."
>
> John 3:27–30

John's words lay out a perfect roadmap for those of us who want to take any part in kingdom work:

Be committed to do what God asks you to do and joyfully give Him the glory for it.

He must increase, and we must decrease.

Warning: Your Business Brain Can Get in the Way

That powerful tool inside your body that God built with incredible precision is hardwired in formulas you've learned at work. You know, like net income = revenue – expenses or profit margin = (net income / revenue) x 100, etc.

So naturally, when you think about increase in the kingdom, your business brain immediately jumps to basic growth principles. And on that route, we quickly arrive at conclusions like:

The bigger my audience is, the more I can do for God.

The better the title I have at work, the more influence I will have for God.

The more others make of me, the more I can make of Christ.

But career and business strategies don't change the fundamentals of our faith. And at its core, kingdom work is wrapped up in His agenda and His glory. Not yours. Not mine.

Let me say it as plainly as I can: You don't have to increase in order for Him to increase.

God doesn't need your business/title/platform/audience to grow to bring Him more glory. He just needs your faith to grow.

Can you be known and still prioritize knowing God? Absolutely.

If your audience grows, can God use that for His glory? Yes!

If you get a promotion at work so you have more influence over more people, can He use you in your new role? Absolutely, God can!

But He's not limited to those means. God's increase is in no shape, form, or fashion, dependent on your increase.

Ditch the Dual Increase

Before we go any further, as promised, we're not here to success shame. If you have a leadership position at work, a résumé full of career accomplishments, or a large social media platform with an engaged audience, that doesn't automatically mean you're in the wrong.

But look at your actions, your motives, and your thought patterns.

Are you trying to increase . . . to make Him increase? Or are you actively seeking ways to get out of the way and elevate Him? Because it's not possible to do both.

There are many routes to destruction, and not all of them exist in a form that is obviously bad. Destruction can come simply from giving more time and attention to the success of your own legacy than to the cause of Christ.

I believe a large portion of stress in kingdom work is rooted in the desire of dual increase:

His mission + my mission.

His agenda + my agenda.

His name + my name.

Imagine what it would be like if you were solely focused on His increase. If you took all of those growth requirements away, what would that mean for you?

No more pressure to be the best.

To sell more than her.

To get more followers.

To have everyone think you're awesome.

Answer honestly: Would your life look drastically different than it does now?

Here's the good news: that's not just some dreamy far-off wishful thinking. That's exactly how we are supposed to live! That pressure doesn't come from God. We've put it on ourselves.

And without even realizing it, the dual increase creates another problem. Thinking too much of ourselves can cause us to think too little of God and too little of others.

Where the Gap Goes

Visually, it may even look something like this:

But God is not just a little above you and me. He is infinitely greater: "'For my thoughts are not your thoughts, neither are your ways my ways,' declares the Lord. 'As the heavens are higher than the earth, so are my ways higher than your ways and my thoughts than your thoughts'" (Isaiah 55:8–9 NIV).

The space between the heavens and the earth is a giant gap, and that's exactly the image God paints for us here. We're not just a little less holy than He is, a little less intelligent than He is, a little less capable than He is, or a little less worthy of praise.

I can't say it better than C. S. Lewis does:

> In God you come against something which is in every respect immeasurably superior to yourself. Unless you know God as that—and, therefore, know yourself as nothing in comparison—you do not know God at all. As long as you are proud you cannot know God. A proud man is always looking down on things and people: and, of course, as long as you are looking down, you cannot see something that is above you.[1]

If we become consumed with growing our position to be known by others, the largest gap starts to go between us and others instead of us and God. And I'll be completely honest: In the social media and promotion culture we live in, it's easier than ever before to welcome (and want!) the large gap between ourselves and others rather than to avoid it. And if there's any lesson we can learn from celebrity culture, elevating someone to a status far above everyone else typically does more damage than good.

This is where the gap should go:

The giant gap goes between God and people collectively. God over us should be the only hierarchy that exists among believers. He created us to work as a unit, giving us different strengths and functions[1] so that we can use our gifts to serve one another.[2] As we go, we are making disciples,[3] encouraging one another and building one another up,[4] considering how to stir up one another to love and good works,[5] bearing one another's burdens,[6] and sharpening one another.[7] Viewing Him rightly sets us up to view ourselves and others rightly.

He Knows Me

J. I. Packer's book *Knowing God* is one of my favorite resources to recommend when someone wants to know how and why we know God, the attributes of God, and why knowing Him matters. And in an entire book devoted to the importance of knowing God, this truth is still the one that blows my mind:

"What matters supremely, therefore, is not, in the last analysis, the fact that I know God, but the larger fact which underlies it—the fact that **he knows me**" (emphasis added).[2]

The very fact that knowing God is even possible for me has nothing to do with my intellect or my discipline. But it has everything to do with the fact that "if anyone loves God, he is known by God."[8]

It all starts with God, and it all ends with God. Why would we make the in-between any different?

1. 1 Corinthians 12.
2. 1 Peter 4:10.
3. Matthew 28:19.
4. 1 Thessalonians 5:11.
5. Hebrews 10:24.
6. Galatians 6:2.
7. Proverbs 27:17.
8. 1 Corinthians 8:3.

Defining Decrease

Humility might be one of the most misunderstood concepts in Christianity. It's not really something that can be mastered. (Once you think you've got it, you've lost it!)

But consistently, Scripture points out that humility is not just something we pray for, but it's an action we must earnestly pursue:

> Do nothing from selfish ambition or conceit, but in humility, count others more significant than yourselves.
>
> Philippians 2:3

> Humble yourselves before the Lord, and he will exalt you.
>
> James 4:10

> Humble yourselves, therefore, under the mighty hand of God so that at the proper time he may exalt you.
>
> 1 Peter 5:6

One of my favorite examples of the pursuit of humility is that of the apostle Paul, which was first pointed out to me by Eric Geiger in his book *How to Ruin Your Life*.[3]

Paul's letters give us an in-depth look at the progression of how the apostle Paul perceived himself. If we examine the letters Paul wrote in chronological order, this is how Paul's view of himself evolved over time:

- *"I am the least of the apostles"*[9]
- *"me—the least of all the saints"*[10]

9. 1 Corinthians 15:9
10. Ephesians 3:8 CSB

- *"'Christ Jesus came into the world to save sinners'—and I am the worst of them"*[11]

Don't miss this: Paul went from seeing himself as the least of the Christian leaders of his time to the least of all believers and finally, to the worst of all sinners.

Paul's view of himself appears to decrease, but on paper, in terms of his "Christian résumé" Paul really had nowhere to go but up. Remember, Paul first encountered Jesus on the road with plans to continue his persecution of Christians. The first person to be martyred for believing in Jesus was a man named Stephen, and Paul (known then as Saul), was the one who watched over the cloaks of the men who stoned him.[12]

But Paul had a radical conversion and gave his life to Christ; he spent the rest of his days proclaiming the Gospel and led many to faith in Christ. The more Paul knew of Christ, the more accurately he could view himself. And his perception of himself had nothing to do with his own accomplishments but rested on what Jesus accomplished on the cross.

Make this a practice in your own life: Refuse to see yourself apart from what Jesus did. Accomplishments and accolades don't just pale in comparison, but at the foot of the cross, vanity vanishes.

Refuse to see yourself apart from what Jesus did.

Back to why humility is often misunderstood: Humility is not weakness or lack of ambition. When we look at a map of Paul's missionary journeys and read the passion in his thirteen letters in the New Testament, it would be easy to conclude that he was arguably the most driven evangelist of all time.

11. 1 Timothy 1:15 CSB
12. Acts 7:58

But it was his perception of Jesus that drove him—not Paul's opinion of himself.

Living to decrease doesn't mean that you disappear or that your life doesn't have meaning.

But living to decrease does mean that our pursuits are motivated by what Christ has done for us, not by what we can do.

She Unfollowed Us + God Still Got to Her

At SWHW, we're committed to sharing truth. But the truth doesn't always feel good, so almost every day on our social media platforms, both on our personal accounts and the ministry account, we see followers come and go. Some days, a lot more go than come.

Not everyone explains why they decide to unfollow, but this woman did, and it rocked me in the best way:

> I felt led to message you this morning. For a while last year, I unfollowed you and SWHW. See, I love personal development and self help, the idea that I can be better each day with my own effort. So you kept saying things that pointed out my sin and my weaknesses and made me question the people that I looked up to. And I didn't like it. So I avoided your message. **But thankfully, I couldn't avoid God.** He has been whispering to me over the last several months, reminding me that it's not about me. Teaching me the great deception of self. His whispers were gentle enough to make me crave more of him, but never condemning. My faith is deepening and I wanted to thank you for planting the seed that I desperately needed.[4]

She avoided my message, but she couldn't avoid God. God didn't need me to get His message to her heart. He knew her, and she knew Him. And that was enough.

So to the one reading who feels personally responsible for everyone around you, I so get you. The burden is real. The life God has called you to live and the influence He has given you matters.

But He matters so much more.

Even if they unfollow you.

Even if your influence doesn't get as big in size as you feel it is in importance.

God isn't limited in who He can reach by the size of your reach.

He doesn't need you to increase so He can increase.

He must increase, and we must decrease.

We must be women who pursue knowing God (because He knows us!) more than we aim to be known.

A Prayer of Personal Decrease + Kingdom Increase

Father, You alone are worthy of my worship.
May my head, my heart, and my hands respond to all You are.
Keep me in awe of Your majesty every moment,
With incessant wonder and amazement that my Creator knows me.[13]

Everything begins with You, God,
And You have already orchestrated the end.
Meet me here in the middle,
And help me feel Your presence as clearly as I can see Your creation.

Keep my gaze on You,
And show me deeper parts of who You are each day.
Make me increasingly aware of the giant gap that exists between You and me.
Make my dependence on You obvious to everyone around me.

Motivate me by what Jesus has done,
Not simply by what I can do.
Replace the pressure to be known by the world,
With overwhelming peace that I know You.

Forgive me when I make other things bigger than I make You.
Especially forgive me when I elevate myself and my own importance.

13. Psalm 139:13.

Help me fight against my pride,
So my pride doesn't fight against my kingdom impact.

Destroy my efforts that are rooted in selfish ambition.
Erase my desire to have any part of the glory that belongs only to You.
Expose my motives and abolish every stronghold.
Take every thought I have that sets itself up against You,
And make it obey Christ.[14]

Help me hunger for humility.
You must increase, Lord,
And I must decrease.[15]
Rewire my brain to know I do not need to increase to make You increase.
Focus my energy on Your increase alone.

I'm willing to plant, and I'm willing to water,
But I know You are the One who gives growth.[16]
So grow my faith, Lord.
And use my life to point others to You.

Amen.

14. 2 Corinthians 10:4–5.
15. John 3:30.
16. 1 Corinthians 3:6.

5

Obedience

Success

Somer

God has been trying to teach humans that true success only comes from our obedience to Him since the beginning of time: Eve, Noah, Jonah, Saul, David, and down the list. Despite all the examples we have, both when they got it right and when they got it wrong, the battle between success and obedience continues.

Our main issue isn't with understanding that following God equals success—most Christians do not disagree with that statement. It is believing that following God is the only definition of success.[1]

You see, we want success by both God's standards and the world's standards. And we have justified pursuing both in our

1. John 15:5.

heads so well. I mean, why wouldn't God be okay with our striving for worldly success? After all, can't we be of greater use to Him if we have achieved more, made more, or been followed by more?

That's just not how He works, though. And I get that it's really hard to believe because this is probably one of the most countercultural truths we're fighting to help you see in this book. But you need to know this: Everything that you've been told makes you successful in this life is nothing more than dirty rags to God:

"All of us have become like one who is unclean, and all our righteous acts are like filthy rags; we all shrivel up like a leaf, and like the wind our sins sweep us away" (Isaiah 64:6 NIV).

To be fair, Christians misinterpret this passage a lot. This does not

- *disparage the real fruit in our life or*
- *mean that no matter what we do, we can never please God.*

Rather, it's not the good works of the Holy Spirit in our lives that are the filthy rags, but the so-called good works of the spiritually dead, aka the fake Christians, that God despises. In other words, when we work in our own power for our own purpose, we might as well be getting paid in dirty laundry as far as God is concerned.

Before we go any further, let me share a few simple but powerful things God has taught me as I've asked Him to give me a kingdom mindset about success.

1. This is a radical concept. Even though you may be used to hearing it and may even think you have it down, learning not to chase worldly success will be one of the most challenging things you ever do in your Christian walk—especially if you're a natural go-getter!

2. God can do far more with a humble heart and willing hands than He can do with your bonus good works (dirty laundry). You don't need to add to His plan.
3. Sometimes, dare I say most times, God's way will not make sense to anyone else. Keep going.
4. God is pleased by your kingdom obedience, not by your earthly merits, but He still expects you to use and multiply your earthly merits for His glory.

Take a moment and ask God to help you empty yourself of what you "know" so that you can redefine success—not just in your head, but in your heart—for what it really is: obedience to your heavenly Father's plan for your life. Nothing more and nothing less.

Because getting this right really can change everything for you.

Warning #1: A False Picture of Success

I can't be the only one who has been scrolling Instagram only to get sucked in by a beautiful image of a #designyourlife entrepreneur on her yacht on a Tuesday with a caption like this:

"So glad I was courageous enough to quit the 9–5 and choose a life of freedom. Truly living out my passion!"

Well, yeah! I'd be passionate about weekday yachting too. Sign me up for that gig, please.

Disclaimer: You will not find us beating up on successful people at She Works HIS Way or anywhere in these pages. There's nothing wrong with taking the yacht out on a Tuesday if that's the life God has blessed you with. However, for a very long time the world has told us that this is how success should look, and now we have social media to literally show us how it looks so that we can compare.

It's just so dangerous.

You see, your success will not always look like her success, which means a yacht might not ever be a form of transportation for you. Bummer, I know. But we have to be very careful about getting sucked into this type of comparison because if we can't compare our successes, then we probably shouldn't try comparing our provision or blessings.

And while I've opened the can anyway, the particular way in which God decides to provide for you or bless you has zero to do with how valuable you are to Him. He doesn't grade or measure by the same standards we do. To Him, a yacht isn't a better blessing than being able to pay your light bill.

Success isn't necessarily fueled by passion, defined by status, or related to your level of freedom. That mindset will most likely leave you frustrated and feeling like a failure. Because in any given moment, there will always be someone who is more excited than you, who has achieved more than you, or who has greater opportunity or flexibility than you do.

So why do I feel like I have to warn you about this gal and her probably very innocent yacht post? Because it's rare to see an ER night-shift nurse or a high school English teacher post a picture that says, "So glad I'm here instead of on a dumb yacht!" But I bet some of them are scrolling past her post, wondering if they've made a big mistake by not choosing the "life of freedom." A saying never so true as it is now on social media: The grass really isn't always greener on the other side. Especially if the other side requires you to go AWOL on God's plan for your life.

True freedom only comes from true obedience.

If God is calling you to a new career or giving you a new assignment, it's definitely okay to accept it! But if not, it's also very okay to stay right where you are. Staying doesn't mean you're not courageous. On the contrary, staying can mean you're called too. Be careful not to always be looking for more or for what's next. That's a very easy way to miss what God is doing in and through you where you are now.

Warning #2: Designed vs. Denied

Several years ago, I owned a fitness studio I was super passionate about, Kent was a pastor at a growing church that we loved, and the girls were in high school involved in all the things. We were super busy, but super content. We had a beautiful home, I drove a soccer-mom minivan, and we had wonderful friends. #designedlife

Be careful not to always be looking for more or for what's next.

But I knew something was coming. There was a heaviness we were all feeling, and it was not comfortable. Do you ever feel that way? God was preparing our hearts for something, and we had no idea what it was.

One morning, after teaching a 5 AM class at our gym, Kent and I sat in the driveway of our home and had a long talk. We committed to praying and asking God to reveal what it was He wanted us to see. Honestly, things got worse before they got better, and what followed was the weirdest season in which our entire family just felt off. Tension was high, and I specifically started feeling a burden that I couldn't exactly put my finger on, but it felt familiar.

God slowly began answering our prayers, but not with the whole story. It was a conversation here, a door opening there, and a series of little things that led up to our discovery of what He was doing. Eventually, we realized God was calling us to another church, and we were in the strangest place of both excitement and grief.

Excitement to finally have an answer and grief because I didn't want to move. I wanted both God's plan and my family's comfort.

Side note: Remember that familiar burden I was feeling? As only God could orchestrate, my burden was familiar because the church God was calling us to was a church we had loved and prayed for from afar for a very long time, but never considered serving at because this church is pastored by my brother. But even in the clarity of the calling and the overwhelming burden for people I had never met but had prayed for, my flesh fought me the whole way.

The American dream, this studio that I had put blood, sweat, and tears into with members who felt like family—was I really just going to leave them?

Kent had a student ministry with so many kids whom we cared for like our own. What would happen to them?

Our church was in the process of building after six years of meeting in a middle school. Were we really going to miss out on what we had all prayed and worked so hard for?

Eventually, I was able to wrap my head around all those hard questions and give them to God. But there was one question that was still haunting me: What will this do to my kids?

I had a sophomore and a senior who were halfway through their school year. They had friends they loved, jobs they enjoyed, and so many people around them who had become like bonus aunts, uncles, and grandparents. Were we really just going to pick them up and move them away?

Then, sitting in church one Sunday morning, our pastor was preaching about Abraham, and sure enough we were walking through the part of his story where God asks Abraham to sacrifice Isaac.[2] Kent and I made eye contact (but not for long, since I was barely keeping it together).

2. Genesis 22.

And then our pastor read this:

> When they came to the place of which God had told him, Abraham built the altar there and laid the wood in order and bound Isaac his son and laid him on the altar, on top of the wood.
>
> Genesis 22:9

Just in case you've never read this before, the story ends with God telling Abraham he did not have to sacrifice his son. But the point is, Abraham was willing. He trusted God enough to do what He asked.

And we wanted to trust God too. So right then, God spoke to both of us and said, "Put them on the altar."

So we did.

And in doing so, we received a lot of "suggestions." Suggestions such as Kent and I living separately until Kennedi graduated. A few families offered for the girls to live with them for the rest of the school year. Members at our studio, especially those who weren't believers, had so many questions and truly were struggling with the idea that we were leaving them.

None of the suggestions and ideas we were given were new to us. No one mentioned anything that hadn't already kept me awake at night or that I wasn't already wrestling with. I had taken all of the same ideas and excuses to God.

But it didn't change what He wanted from us. So we didn't change our plans.

Some people still didn't get it. Well-intentioned, loving people who genuinely cared about us. And honestly, I understood. We were all trying to negotiate with God, and that just doesn't work. Ever.

So years later, here's my response to the negotiation approach we so often want to take when God asks us to obey but it doesn't feel like it will lead to success. Or when He calls us to do something that's really countercultural and sacrificial in front of our kids (and really any non-believer watching from the outside).

Won't it be terribly difficult to teach our children or show our friends we have to obey God over culture if we don't do what God asks us to do when He asks us to do it, even if it's difficult?

Delayed obedience is disobedience, and as a mom, I'm definitely not qualified to argue with God on the subject of what's best for my kids.

Obedience over success isn't just something power-hungry adults who have workaholic tendencies need to understand. It's something we all need to understand, and the older we are when we learn it, the harder it is to change our thinking!

I know that not all of you reading this book are parents. But for those of you who are or who plan to be someday, please hear me, because this is critical:

If you are consumed with your child's athletic career or academic performance, with making them a star, helping boost their social status, or achieving anything else you've grabbed onto as an idol on their behalf, please be warned! Whatever you're prioritizing for them, you're teaching them that's what matters most. I was super into all those things too, and probably the best soccer mom you'll ever meet, but then God said GO, so we had to go. #deniedlife

I get the pressure you feel to make sure you don't ruin your child's life. I understand you want them to feel safe and secure, and to have all the chances in the world to be great at something. But if they're not great at following God, their other greats will be all they will ever have, and right now is the best life will ever be for them.

They'll go on to live a safe life, maybe even a good life, chasing after success, but never understanding their true purpose. Never knowing the joy and fulfillment that comes when they chase Jesus above all else, because that's not what you showed them was most important.

I'm so sorry if this stings—it stung me too! But I'm so grateful to know this now, because a life of obedience is actually the good life, and I don't want you (or your kids!) to miss out on the real good life because you're stuck chasing the world's fraudulent version of it.

I had no idea what would happen to my kids, or any of us for that matter, if we took this risk and uprooted ourselves at a rather odd time in our lives.

But I knew that God knew, and that was more than enough for me.

You see, it's His job to know and my job to obey. When God and I are working together rightly, that's how success is experienced.

I love the way Elisabeth Elliot puts it:

> God is God. If He is God, He is worthy of my worship and my service. I will find rest nowhere but in His will, and that will is infinitely, immeasurably, unspeakably beyond my largest notions of what He is up to.[1]

As I look back on this transition we went through as a family, I realize now, in the grand scheme of things, that this wasn't a huge deal. People move all of the time. But for our family, it was transformational because when God proves His faithfulness, in big or small ways, it changes us.

This move changed us. I have been blown away by the spiritual maturity I've seen in my girls since that move. It certainly didn't happen overnight, and there were low moments between the high ones, but they both would tell you that they learned to trust God in a much deeper way than ever before, because they also experienced God's presence in a more personal way than ever before. And that's the ultimate goal for Kent and me—that our kids will grow to love God so much that they will not need to depend on our faith because they have their own.

And we will forever tell this story in hopes that it will give you or whoever hears it courage to look culture in the face and say: I will not follow you. I will not be influenced by you. I will not feel bad because I don't look like you. And, if I'm a parent, I certainly will not feel guilty raising children who don't do what you tell them to do.

God's way is different. So, so different! We embraced the denied life, and we got abundance.[3] Abundant joy, abundant peace, abundant adventure![4]

Trust me: You will never be able to design anything better than what He has for you. Lay it all down and let Him lead.[5]

God's Standard for Success

Measurements. Metrics. Performance Evaluation. If you're here, I'm betting you love them.

Rightfully so. In the work world, measurables play a big role in helping us determine what's successful and what's not, where to invest more and where to pull back, etc. And while there's certainly nothing wrong with loving measurables, our spiritual success in life can't be quantified on the same scales we use at work.

Matthew 25:14–30 is a passage we can use to understand the truth about what God sees as success. (I encourage you to pop your Bible open and read the verses for yourself, then meet me back here for some application.)

In summary, though, here's what happens:

3. John 10:10
4. Romans 15:13
5. Ephesians 3:20–21.

You will never be able to design anything better than what He has for you. Lay it all down and let Him lead.

Jesus is sharing a parable about a master who is going on a long trip. Before the master leaves, he divvies up some of his property to his servants. The master determines how much he gives each servant according to their ability (one gets five talents, one gets two talents, and one gets one talent), and he goes on his way. When he returns, the master checks in with each servant for an account of what he entrusted to them.

Two of the servants receive fantastic feedback for doubling their master's resources:

> His master replied, "Well done, good and faithful servant! You have been faithful with a few things; I will put you in charge of many things. Come and share your master's happiness!"
>
> Matthew 25:21, 23 NIV

But one servant didn't take any action with what his master entrusted to him. He returns to the master what is his; instead of doing something with it, he had merely buried the money in the ground.

The master called this man a "wicked, lazy servant,"[6] scolding him for not at least putting the money in the bank so it could have accrued interest while he was away. Then the master takes the one talent from the wicked and lazy servant and gives it to the servant who had ten talents.

Don't miss the big picture here. God reveals something really special to us through this parable. We now know how He measures success: good and faithful or wicked and lazy.

6. Matthew 25:26 NIV.

God doesn't grade on a curve. He doesn't play favorites. At the end of our lives, God will either deem us good and faithful or wicked and lazy. There are no other options.

Obedience looks like good and faithful service: What am I doing with what God has given me, and how much glory is He getting from it?

Disobedience looks like wicked and lazy service: How little can I get by with doing, or how much glory am I going to get from this?

The measurements you choose to use reveal whose kingdom you're here to build. Yours or His?

Friend, God will not bless your kingdom. His kingdom come, His will be done[7]—that is success. We can be a part of it, or we can fight against it, but none of us can be neutral.

It Boils Down to This

There is a glaring difference between the one-talent servant and the five- and two-talent servants: entrusted vs. excuses.

When the servants with five and two talents spoke to their master, they both began with, "You entrusted [five/two] talents to me."[8]

The one-talent servant, though, began with an excuse: "I knew that you are a hard man, harvesting where you have not sown and gathering where you have not scattered seed. So I was afraid and went out and hid your gold in the ground. See, here is what belongs to you."[9]

Our response, whether we pursue being good and faithful by way of godly ambition or we give in to the temptation to be

7. Matthew 6:10.
8. Matthew 25:20, 22 NASB.
9. Matthew 25:24–25 NIV.

passively inactive and settle for wicked and lazy, really has to do with how we view God.

The same goes for success. We will view success rightly when we view God rightly.

- *Are you like the five- and two-talent servants, viewing Him as a loving, giving God who has entrusted you with something?*
- *Or do you view God as hard and unfair, as the one-talent servant did, believing what you do or don't do doesn't really matter to Him?*

Honestly, the words of the one-talent servant that might break my heart the most are "Here is what belongs to you." This servant chose fear over faithfulness. He was afraid that somehow he would disappoint his master, so he chose to do nothing, frozen in fear, instead.

Please remember that God is not after your performance. He is after your heart. And when He gets your heart, obedience is inevitable. Growth cannot be stunted. You will be more than just successful, you'll be victorious.[10]

Yes, God's work matters. Attaching His name to our lives calls us to the highest standard—but that is more about your obedience than your ability.

Following God is not a performance. But obedience is active, not passive.

That's why the master says, "Well **done**, my good and faithful servant," emphasis added.

Not well planned.

Not well intentioned.

Not well conceived.

Well done.

10. Romans 8:37.

And here is why this matters so much. This parable isn't merely an allegory. One day, we will all stand before a holy God and give an account of our lives. And He won't be asking us how much money we made or how many followers we had on Instagram.

It will simply be: Do you know Him, and were you obedient with what He gave you?

Well done, good and faithful servant.

That is what we're working for.

That is success.

Nothing more. Nothing less.

A Prayer to Pursue Success as Obedience

Father, give me a humble heart and willing hands.
Channel my ambition for Your kingdom alone.
Do not let me be fooled by the world's false promises and empty claims.
Increase my confidence that real freedom is only found in You.

Forgive me whenever I chase worldly success over simple obedience.
Help me to pursue what I should be busy with right now before pursuing what's next,
And let my actions prove me to be faithfully ready for Your next assignment.
Overwhelm me with passion to pursue Your plan for my life.

Make Your desires my desires.

No matter the task, help me wake up each morning,
Thrilled to be doing the work that You have called me to.
Establish my every step.[11]
Make me content in Your presence, not the final destination.

When I become restless because I'm ready for something new . . .

Help me to not grow weary in doing good,[12]

11. Psalm 119:133.
12. Galatians 6:9.

But to remain steadfast, working hard in the place
where you have me,[13]
For the people you have around me.[14]

When I become bored because I'm ready for something
more exciting . . .

Help me to remember You can abundantly exceed my
ambition and imagination.[15]
You are able to do a new thing in the same place and in
forgotten places.[16]
"Here I am! Send me."[17]

When I become discontent because I'm not getting
enough credit or recognition . . .

Remind me my goal is for people to overlook me
because they see You.
Show me Your glory, Lord,
So I can glorify You before others.

Show me the next step.
Give me the faith to follow,
The courage to stay,
The motivation to work hard,
And the boldness to glorify You.

Amen.

13. Colossians 3:23.
14. 1 Peter 4:10.
15. Ephesians 3:20.
16. Isaiah 43:19.
17. Isaiah 6:8.

6

You

Me

Michelle

Culture says: Look out for yourself first.

God says: Consider others as more important than yourself.

My nickname as a kid was Motormouth. (I talked a lot. Not much has changed.)

My nickname now: Purpose Police. (I can turn a budget meeting into a sermon.)

Nicknames make us laugh, but there's usually a story or some truth behind the nicknames we're given, right? Nicknames are earned.

Perhaps no one earned a better nickname than a man named Joseph during the growth of the early church. The apostles called him Barnabas, which means "son of encouragement."[1]

1. Acts 4:36.

That means Joseph was such an encourager that he was better known for being an encourager than for being Joseph.

When we first meet Barnabas, he's laying his profit from selling a piece of land at the apostles' feet.[2] And while that's incredible, in my mind, that's only a small glimpse into what makes him a kingdom legend.

But before we go there you need to know this: Barnabas hasn't always been my hero. In fact, I followed Christ for many years before I heard his story. And even when I did, I glossed over it pretty quickly. My attention immediately went to Paul. You know, the apostle Paul. As in arguably the greatest missionary of all time. The author of the majority of the New Testament. A man so committed to Christ that not even prison stays, shipwrecks, or snake bites could stop his passion for the Gospel.

Paul quickly became one of my Bible favorites. And beyond that, being called to ministry, I wanted to be Paul. I mean, who wouldn't want to leave that kind of impact behind? So in my mid-twenties, I did a deep dive into Paul's life. And that was when I uncovered that it was Barnabas who first took a chance on Paul and played a huge role in the lasting legacy of his ministry.

In case you've never paid much attention to Barnabas, I want to walk through his story so you can see how the Lord convicted me that while there's certainly nothing wrong with aspiring to live for Christ with the same passion as Paul, life may offer us more opportunities to be like Barnabas than it presents to be Paul. And because incredible kingdom impact is not limited to what is known and noteworthy, we can't miss our Barnabas moments. We can't miss the moments to live you (others) before me.

2. Acts 4:37.

Barnabas's Big Risk

Let's start with Paul's beginnings. Before he was Paul, the great missionary, he was Saul, a man who personally persecuted Christians, an up-and-coming leader among those responsible for the death of Jesus.[3]

But God. On his way to Damascus, with the ultimate goal to capture, threaten, and murder disciples of the Lord, Saul encounters Jesus instead. And instead of killing Christians, Paul converts to Christianity himself. Shortly after, Paul begins preaching and proclaiming Jesus. Paul, now a preacher, makes his way to Jerusalem and wants to meet up with the disciples, but they "were all afraid of him, for they did not believe that he was a disciple."[4]

It all seems to happen quickly in Acts 9, but Galatians 1:12–18 clears up the timeline for us. When Paul attempts to meet with the disciples, it has been three years since his conversion. And during those three years, he has done nothing but partner with them in the Gospel from afar.

But Paul's past still posed a risk. And in the defense of the disciples, there were plenty of facts to back up their judgment and reservations. Thankfully, though, there was Barnabas the encourager, who had all the same facts, and yet chose faith instead. Barnabas brought Paul to the apostles and declared his testimony to them. And with the endorsement of Barnabas, the disciples' fear turned to acceptance, and Paul began preaching in Jerusalem as one of them.[5]

Self-Reflection: Do you suppose you would have been like Barnabas, willing to risk your reputation to offer Paul a second chance? Or would you have been more like the disciples—fearful, skeptical, and more prone to play it safe?

3. Acts 9:1-2.
4. Acts 9:1–26.
5. Acts 9:27–28.

I admit it: I understand the disciples' hesitation. I probably would have been fearful too. But love doesn't play it safe. And love is how Jesus summarized all of the law: loving God and loving others.[6] It's easy to wear Love God, Love Others on a T-shirt, but living this out isn't nearly as quick, easy, convenient, or even normal.

We live the Gospel vertically by putting God over everything. But we're also called to live the Gospel horizontally as His witnesses. We live the Gospel horizontally by putting you before me.

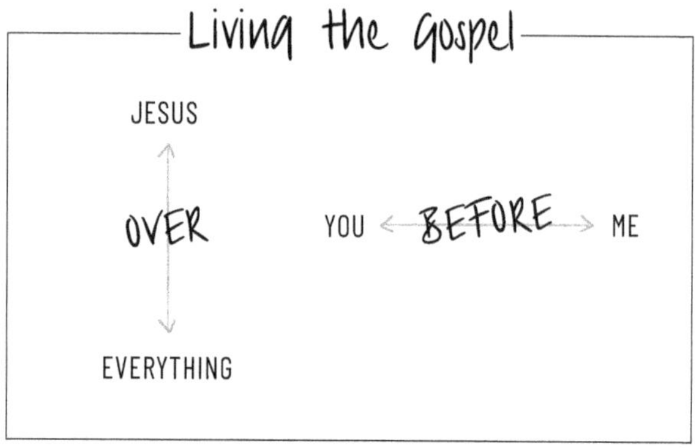

That's what Barnabas did for Paul. Just as Jesus, our sinless Savior, died the death we deserved and put you and me before himself, Barnabas was willing to sacrifice his own comfort and potentially his credibility when he advocated for Paul.

Be Believers

Picture it. I imagine there were gasps as the disciples physically moved away from the door when Paul walked in. Given their

6. Matthew 22:36–40.

fear, I highly doubt it was a warm welcome, which makes Barnabas's speaking up instead of shrinking back even more notable.

It's much easier to endorse someone after they've been endorsed by someone else. But genuine belief isn't afraid to go first. Everyone else feared, but Barnabas believed. And not just a quiet "I believe in you" whispered in Paul's ear. Barnabas brought Paul to the apostles and affirmed him publicly.

Do you remember the first person who took a chance on you? Someone who believed in you before you established credibility? The one who was further along and took the time to take you with them? If it has happened to you, of course you do. It's devastatingly rare, so those leaders are forever etched in our memories.

I remember . . .

- *Dr. Thomas White, who hired me as a writer after I'd already quit one job working for him in the admissions office.*
- *Chalene Johnson who told me, "Put faith and fitness together; don't keep them separate. It's who you are."*
- *Mark and Pat Cooper, who took James and me to dinner almost weekly when we were barely making it financially, newly married, and finishing school. Our mentoring dinners typically ran so long that the employees at Jason's Deli got used to sweeping the floor after closing while we finished up.*
- *Teeny Pineda, who quit the reliable job that she loved to be my assistant because the addition of She Works HIS Way was too much for me to manage alone.*
- *Clayton and Sharie King, who invited James and me to crash their anniversary dinner when we were merely acquaintances because we were coming off of several really difficult decisions and they wanted to encourage us.*

I could list more people who have put my interests before their own, who lived out you before me to my benefit. However, the more I work with others, the more I realize that stories like mine are not common. Many people I encounter have never been encouraged. They've never been challenged. They've never been mentored. And this often leads to their feeling that they don't matter.

Courage often follows belief. I think it's why the "believe in yourself" mantra is so rampant. Because it is not common practice to profess and act on our belief in one another, the default belief has become that in order to achieve something, you have to believe in yourself—because if you don't, no one else will.

Believers (yes, I'm reminding us what we call one another), we must do better! Believe in God. And also believe in one other. God can use your belief as a catalyst for courage among His children. Because, lest we forget, every person is an image-bearer of God[7] and fearfully and wonderfully made.[8] God has planned a hopeful future for His children,[9] and His power at work in us far exceeds human ambition and requests.[10]

You and I don't make people awesome; God has already done that. So we really shouldn't be able to separate believing in God and believing in one another. Belief in a Christ-follower is simply a matter of believing what God can do in them and through them.

For example, David was not the strongest soldier for the battle against Goliath. In fact, David wasn't a soldier at all! He was just a shepherd boy who showed up because he was bringing his brothers a snack at the battle line.[11]

But David knew what God was capable of, so he stepped up when he heard Goliath's taunts. And rather than choosing

7. Genesis 1:27.
8. Psalm 139:14.
9. Jeremiah 29:11.
10. Ephesians 3:20.
11. 1 Samuel 17:15–20.

words of belief and gratitude, Saul reminded David of his youth, likely referring to both his size and his inexperience.[12]

I pray that doesn't sound familiar to you, but because I know the world we live in, I'm sure there are some of you reading who have encountered a version of what Saul told David in your own life:

You are not able to ______________ because you are ______________.

Let me be the voice of truth telling you that neither blank in the above statement is one Jesus cannot fill. This is confidence in Christ not arrogance about our capability—hope that no matter what, He can.

The success formula for a God-sized task is God's power + human willingness, not God's power + human strength or skill.

Don't miss the opportunity to be that belief for someone else. It's a big deal, and it's bigger than merely helping one person. Don't miss being a part of the kingdom of God in this way.

The success formula for a God-sized task is God's power + human willingness, not God's power + human strength or skill.

Limiting your kingdom impact to what you can do marginalizes the legacy it's possible to leave behind. Make it your mission to believe in others so well that your life serves as a catalyst of kingdom courage for many.

Think about it. Who is the you you put before me? (It should be the goal to have many such yous in our life, by the way.) Answer these three questions:

Whom do I believe in?

How do they know I believe in them?

12. 1 Samuel 17:32–33.

How do I show I believe in them?
Repeat as many times as possible.

More Workers > More Work

The story of Barnabas and Paul only begins at his introduction to the disciples. From Acts 9 through 15, these two men become an incredible Gospel duo (a trio, including the Holy Spirit![13]). Miracles. Opposition. Preaching. It's all there. Barnabas accompanies Paul on his first missionary journey. The Gospel spreads, and these two have a front-row seat to the power of God at work.

But then something happens to change this dynamic. Paul wants to go on a second journey to visit the churches they've started. Barnabas agrees and suggests they take Mark with them. But Paul is not having it.

You see, Mark started their first journey with them, but he didn't finish with them. We don't know why, but at a certain point Mark had left them . . . and Paul had not forgotten. The disagreement over whether to include Mark again ultimately results in Paul and Barnabas going separate ways: Paul on a second missionary journey with Silas, and Barnabas on another missionary journey with Mark.[14]

Do you have certain stories in the Bible you really resonate with? I get Paul on a real level here. Loyalty was a big deal to him. So, in a moment of justified mistrust, despite being given a major second chance himself, Paul's grace tank dropped immediately to E, and he refuses to chance letting some homesick mama's boy stop his momentum—even if it meant separating himself from his mentor. (Again, we don't

13. Acts 13:2.
14. Acts 15:39.

know for sure why Mark left. I'm just making guesses over here!)

Personally, I've done this wrong more times than I care to count. Especially when the task at hand is a kingdom endeavor, I can attempt to justify the means to the end quickly. But here's what I've learned: If the purpose of our work is to work for the glory of God and the good of others, we can't let the goal—yes, even when it's a good and godly thing—cause us to go at such a pace that we miss doing what's best for the people God puts around us.

We never outgrow the basics. Beyond being elementary lessons, basics serve as a solid foundation on which all other instruction builds. Jesus' command is to love God and love others, not merely to love God and love the work. Every genuine kingdom effort is about souls far more than it is about the task.

That's why business is never just business when you're a believer. In your work, from your attitude to your integrity to your actions, in the seen and the unseen, it's always about God and it's always about others: Jesus over everything,[1] and you before me.

Jesus put it plainly to the disciples: There's plenty of work to be done. There's simply not enough workers who are willing to do it.[15] Whenever we find ourselves looking for something to do, we're likely looking for the wrong work.

As Jesus instructed, let's pray for more workers,[16] but let's also actively seek to be part of the solution to our prayers. Who can you find to join you in His work? Who is your you? Or have you become so focused on yourself or the task that you've missed investing in those around you?

15. Matthew 9:37.
16. Matthew 9:38.

Make It Personal

For my fellow dreamers, each time I felt God put an idea in my heart, I used to immediately jump to the question, How will I do this?

At first glance, it's not the worst question, but that mindset puts the focus on my work. Now I ask a new question first: Who will come with me? Followed by, How will we do this?

LOVING GOD AND LOVING THE WORK ASKS:	LOVING GOD AND LOVING OTHERS ASKS:
How will I do this?	Who will come with me and how will we do this?

When you look back someday on the scope of your work, wouldn't you prefer to see it as faces rather than as tasks? Me too. Well, remembering our work in faces someday requires that we must work with faces today.

Paul may have missed his first chance with Mark, but not only did they reconcile (we're getting there), but Paul ended up being extremely personal in the way he did ministry. Just look at the final chapter of Romans. There are thirty-five names tucked into this chapter alone in personal greetings and messages![17]

People are the reason Paul's ministry ended up being so rich. Some 2,000 years later, we're still building upon what he established. Every New Testament letter written and almost every name within it represents workers he recruited. And I can't help

17. Romans 16.

but think that Barnabas's example was one of the reasons Paul prioritized people the way he did.

More workers is the goal. Not merely more work for ourselves. You before me.

Support More Often than You Star

Barnabas never sought the spotlight. That doesn't mean he was never in it, but the spotlight wasn't the goal. And despite sometimes finding his way to the center of attention, he was just as comfortable being in the background.

Think about it: Barnabas put in the energy and effort to affirm Paul and help him get started. Then, instead of continuing what he helped start with Paul and moving up the ranks in importance, he chose to give Mark a second chance. Once again, Barnabas started over in order to build up someone else. Paul's reputation as a Christian-killer didn't stop Barnabas from taking a chance on him, and neither did Mark's reputation as a flight risk.

While we don't get to read about the reconciliation between Paul and Barnabas, we do know Mark didn't finish ministry as a quitter. In later letters, Paul records that Mark was being helpful to him in his ministry.[18] But Mark's story doesn't end there. Most biblical scholars agree that Mark's gospel account was the first of the four written.

Let that sink in. The first detailed narrative of the life of Jesus was penned by Mark. Mark went from abandoning a mission to being God's chosen man to first write what Jesus did on earth. And once again, the person who took the time to invest in him before it made sense was Barnabas.

So hang on. Mark is credited with one of the four written gospel accounts. The majority of the world even outside of

18. 2 Timothy 4:11.

Christianity has at least heard of the apostle Paul. And Barnabas is ultimately the one God used to empower both of their ministries. Yet there are a lot of Christ-followers who don't know much, if anything, about Barnabas.

Yep. Barnabas was willing to mentor two people (that we know of) who ultimately would outshine him. And to this day, the kingdom is better for it.

Let's remember, friend, it is the world that tries to convince us to finish ahead of others. God only requires that we finish well.[19] Two things can't be first, so if our work always is done with an ulterior motive to finish first, God has lost His rightful place.

It is the world that tries to convince us to finish ahead of others. God only requires that we finish well.

Honesty time: Do you ever waste time exerting energy over getting the credit instead of a unified resolve that God will get the glory? If we truly want it to be about God, it's got to be okay that many times the win or the glory has little or nothing to do with us.

What does that mean for how we interact with others? We should support them and help them however we can to ensure God gets the maximum glory. Sacrificing the spotlight shouldn't even be categorized as a sacrifice because the spotlight shouldn't matter.

A few years ago, as Somer was addressing a group of women who had secular jobs, you could have heard a pin drop when she said, "If God calls you to be a rung on the ladder that your competition climbs, then be sturdy, be strong, and help her up."

She's not your competition. She's not your enemy. She's either your sister in Christ or a woman in need of a Savior. Talk

19. Matthew 25:21, 23.

about a way to help someone who doesn't know Christ see the difference He can make in your life. She may blow off your Bible reading and prayer habits or think that prioritizing church attendance over weekend adventures is weird, but she won't be able to ignore the Gospel when you put her before yourself.

I wish I could say that Christian women do this exponentially better, but we typically don't do it much better than the world does. Or sometimes, even when we get it right, it's often cheapened to an agenda that looks more like feminism than the Gospel. We should build other women up because of Jesus—not simply female empowerment.

What if Christian stereotypes were replaced to reflect this kind of attitude? With comments like

- *She's always there for me, and I don't even know why.*
- *She championed my small contribution so much that I ended up getting more credit than she did.*
- *You definitely want to get to know her. Everyone who works with her leaves better off.*

Wouldn't that make non-believers curious about Christ? Wouldn't the fact that He actually makes a difference in our lives make them pay attention more than consenting to blend in with culture?

That's the you before me mindset. That's the life God calls us to live.

Her Path May Not Be Your Path

It's never fun to dwell on a disagreement. And honestly, I think "What happened between Paul and Barnabas?!" will be one of my first questions when I get to heaven. But despite not knowing the details of how their relationship ended or whether reconciliation between the two ever took place, we can still look back and see how God used their split for His good.

Barnabas took Mark and went to Cyprus. Paul took Silas, and they set off for Syria and Cilicia, "strengthening the churches."[20] What would have been one missionary journey with two missionaries became two missionary journeys with four missionaries.

Christ is the only path to God—Jesus is the Author and Finisher of our faith[21] and Jesus is the Way, the Truth and the Life[22]—but there is not just one path that leads to Christ because God's servants are needed everywhere.

So just because her path doesn't look like your path, that doesn't mean it's not His path.

The same God who called you to delete your Instagram account can call her to start one.

The same God who called you to work outside the home can call her to stay home with her kids.

The same God who called you to make God visible through your ministry can call her to be a light in a secular industry.

And yes—even regarding the person you invested in, poured into, loved, mentored, discipled—God may have put you two together for a season and not forever. God calls us to gather,[23] but He also calls us to go.[24] And ultimately, they're not your people. They're God's people.

Your purpose in investing in someone may be to send them, not to keep them. And considering that God charges us to take His message to the ends of the earth, we probably should be sending far more often than we're keeping.

20. Acts 15:36–41.
21. Hebrews 12:2 KJV.
22. John 14:6.
23. Hebrews 10:24–25.
24. Matthew 10:7; Luke 9:2, 60; Matthew 28:19–20.

Look back at the people you've mentored who have gone on to other things, do you resent them or are you proud of them? There may be rare exceptions when others don't leave well, but if you typically are resentful when someone moves on, that's a me-centered mindset. Usually when something keeps happening over and over, everyone else isn't the problem. It's probably you who needs to change.

For example, Somer quit my network marketing team. It was a good fit for her for a season, but when God called her to lay it down, she did, and I supported her decision. She had complete integrity in how she handled her exit, and although I greatly missed being able to work with her in that way, it didn't affect our friendship. And how sweet is God to have each of us go separate ways only to end up serving Him at She Works HIS Way together?

J. D. Greear put it like this: "God calls his leaders, not to a platform to build a great ministry for themselves, but to an altar where they die unto themselves. This means sending out our best with abandon."[2]

I know it hurts. I know it's not easy. The human response is for me to see what's best for me and for you to do what's best for you, and for neither of us to give an inch. With the argument between Paul and Barnabas, I imagine there was hurt and blame on both sides. But the godly response is to believe what's possible for the kingdom, trusting that God is always working and that His purposes stretch far beyond what we can see or feel in the moment.

Because ultimately, what many may have seen as the end of the ministry of Paul and Barnabas was actually the beginning of the ministry of Paul and Silas and the beginning of ministry for Barnabas and Mark. So even if we don't know how a certain circumstance will turn out, we can trust the results because we trust the One who is in control of it all.

Just do your part, friend. Put others' needs and desires before your own. God will handle the rest.

Empty Yourself

The you-before-me life isn't natural. And again, it's not your responsibility to turn others into something. Everyone is already created in God's image. You're just responsible for living your life for God and others—not for yourself.

I love how Andy Stanley put it: "As leaders, we are never responsible for filling someone else's cup. Our responsibility is to empty ours."[3]

Catch that? The easiest way to live you before me is to empty yourself. To aim to put an end to the me who aims to compete with you.

Paul wrote about this very concept. Really take to heart these words of Philippians 2:3–8 (NIV), in bold:

"Do nothing out of selfish ambition or vain conceit."

Yes, that actually means nothing.

"Rather, in humility value others above yourselves,"

Always treat one another as the more important one.

"not looking to your own interests but each of you to the interests of the others."

It's not just about not looking to your interests, but actively looking to the interests of others.

"In your relationships with one another, have the same mindset as Christ Jesus:"

View others as Christ sees them.

"Who, being in very nature God, did not consider equality with God something to be used to his own advantage;"

If Jesus never tried to pull rank, you and I certainly have no right to do so.

"rather, he made himself nothing by taking the very nature of a servant, being made in human likeness."

Living life like Jesus requires that we stop at nothing short of making ourselves nothing.

"And being found in appearance as a man, he humbled himself by becoming obedient to death—even death on a cross!"

It's not possible to go lower than Jesus went for you, but it would serve others well to live as if you could.

Jesus went first as our example. Now it's our turn.

- *Culture's way of leaving the greatest legacy requires you to outshine everyone around you.*
- *God's way of leaving the greatest legacy requires you to elevate others—even those who will outshine you. (Insecurity is the only reason why you wouldn't.)*
- *Culture encourages investing in people to keep for your own agenda.*
- *God encourages investing in people to send them out for His agenda.*
- *Culture says, "Elevate yourself." And whether it requires you to put someone else down, exaggerate your résumé, or simply go throughout life looking out for your own interests first, somehow, culture will convince you that the end will justify the means.*
- *God says, "Empty yourself." With that as your goal, there will be no need to elevate yourself—because God will do that for you.*[25]

Don't miss that last part because your flesh will definitely try to fool you. Putting others' needs and interests before your own will not leave you last in line. Doing so will make you realize you don't have to scrap and claw to get to the top on your own because you're confident God will take care of you.

Jesus over everything.

You before me.

God will handle the rest.

25. 1 Peter 5:6.

A Prayer to Put Others Before Self

God, I will never be able to fully fathom Your selfless love for me.
But don't let me stop at merely being grateful for it.
Remind me that Your example sets the standard
For the way I am to love others.[26]

Forgive me for the energy I've exerted on desiring credit or attention.
Forgive me for how I struggle to see past myself and my feelings.
Forgive me for building more platforms than altars.
Forgive me for the times I've been resentful of a background role.
Forgive me when I've allowed myself to care more about tasks than about people.

Give me Your eyes to see those around me.
Every person I encounter is known by You,
Formed by You and set apart by You.[27]
Help me believe what You are capable to do in them and through them.
Use me to be a catalyst for kingdom courage.

God, I'm begging You to send more workers for Your mission.[28]
Use me to invest in, help, and support Your workers.
Help me seek souls far more than I seek the spotlight.
Give me instincts to elevate others,

26. John 13:34.
27. Jeremiah 1:5.
28. Luke 10:2.

And the desire to pull out of others what You already put in them.

You've given each of us a gift to serve one another,
And every gift serves as evidence of Your grace in various forms.[29]
Expose my immaturity when my actions show
I am intimidated or jealous of Your grace.
Mature me to be grateful and encouraged when I see You on display in others.

Help me to always treat others as the more important one.
Make me increasingly aware of others' interests.
Whenever I'm tempted to elevate myself,
Help me empty myself instead.
Make me like-minded with Jesus.

Amen.

29. 1 Peter 4:10.

7

Relationships

Achievements

Somer

Introvert or extrovert, it doesn't matter. In today's world, it's a struggle to have a relationship with someone that goes deeper than surface level. Fact: People are hard.

I know I'm difficult. You probably have your moments too. It's extremely tempting to walk head-down through life, avoiding relationships and the undeniable baggage they bring.

But God doesn't want us to do that, so we can't let ourselves just do what's easiest or most convenient.

Not only do we want you to prioritize relationships over achievements, we want you to come to the end of your life and be able to say your greatest achievements were your relationships. Depending on your personality, this call to build relationships and invest in people may take some seriously difficult, mostly uncomfortable, but oh-so-worth-it work on your part.

Let's not forget that the Great Commandment[1] Jesus gave us was not to love God and work really hard. His command is for us to love God and love people.

Born to Be an Achiever

Speaking of working really hard . . . I was born driven with a desire to perform. I remember being in a restaurant as a young girl with my brother and sister when our server said to my parents, "Your children are so well behaved."

I was so proud of myself. Beaming almost.

I learned early on that I could get noticed for my achievements faster than I could get noticed for just being Somer. Think about it: When we introduce ourselves or others, we typically add to their name, either with a title or something we love about them. It's rarely been simply, "This is Somer."

I wanted to make sure that when someone said, "This is Somer," they would be able to follow it up with something great:

> *"my favorite employee . . ." or*
> *"the nicest girl . . ." or*
> *"the one who came up with that really great idea."*

Just Somer was not enough. I preferred Somer + anything awesome.

So I worked to be noticed for my work.

That wasn't really a terrible thing at first. My work ethic and maturity opened up a lot of amazing opportunities for me early in life that I'm extremely grateful I had. But it turns out that work ethic and maturity were just the beginning. These honorable characteristics quickly became harder and harder

1. Matthew 22:35–40.

to control. My flesh took over, and all of a sudden my good work ethic turned me into an overwhelmed workaholic, and my maturity turned into pride.

I was content only when I was winning.

Building achievements became a priority.

Building relationships fell by the wayside.

I am definitely not proud of that. But praise God for friends who pursued me and for His Word, specifically 1 Samuel and the story of Saul, which cut me deeply, right where I needed it.

Let's go there next.

The Last Twenty-Four Hours

Oh, King Saul. A man of great potential, but with too much ego to ever reach it.

My frustration with his story (as if I have any right to be frustrated with a man I have more in common with than I'd like to admit), however, was not so much his ego, but his inability to realize what a big deal it was to be God's anointed king.

Like, wow.

But as jealousy and selfishness became his greatest motivators and loudest feelings, they stole his greatest blessings: relationships with his family, a noble reputation, and God's very special, anointed attention.

Because of that, Saul lived in isolation and fear, only keeping around him those people he could leverage for his good. He was constantly having to watch his back because he was unable to trust anyone.

What a sad life. And it gets worse.

Toward the end of Saul's life, you can almost feel his story darken.[2] In distress over the Philistine army's coming to destroy

2. 1 Samuel 28.

the Israelites, Saul desperately needed someone to talk to. Someone to impart wisdom. Someone to tell him what to do and to assure him that "it's all going to be okay."

But Saul was alone. So alone that he ended up hiring a medium to summon the only man he was ever really able to trust, his one friend, Samuel.

There's just one catch, though. Samuel was dead, which was why he consulted the medium.

Are you kidding me?!

That was pretty much Samuel's reaction too. His first words to Saul were, "Why have you disturbed me by bringing me up?"[3] Not exactly the warmest greeting.

The conversation just gets more uncomfortable from there. Before Samuel departs, he gives Saul some terribly heavy news:

"Moreover, the Lord will give Israel also with you into the hand of the Philistines, and tomorrow you and your sons shall be with me."[4]

Saul was going to die. The next day.

It's morbid, but have you ever thought about what you would do if you had only twenty-four hours left to live? For most of us, I'm guessing our plans would involve the people we love.

But not Saul.

He "fell at once full length on the ground"[5] and lay there, refusing to eat or drink until the medium basically forced food in him. Saul has twenty-four hours left to live, and he spends the majority of it on the floor, in a stranger's home, whining.

Saul had a list of great achievements, but he did not have a list of great relationships. I can't help but feel bad for him.

3. 1 Samuel 28:15.
4. 1 Samuel 28:19.
5. 1 Samuel 28:20.

Being lonely is hard enough, but being a lonely leader is both hard and dangerous.

We have to be a friend to have a friend, which requires outward focus and inward humility. Frankly, that's not natural for a lot of us, but praise be to God that we have the power of His Holy Spirit to make us better at it. Let's not forget that in all things, not just relationships, what does not come naturally for humans can come supernaturally by way of our God who loves us.

Let me make this really clear for the busy, the shy, the introvert, and the socially awkward like me: We don't get out of being in community just because our preference is solitude. Don't get me wrong, because there is a time and a place for each. I know I'm better in community when I've had my time to hide, but we must not hide from the gift of friendship forever.

Friends are important, and here is how I came to realize that on a deep level.

BFFs

I would never have described myself as someone without friendships. I mean, I had a husband and two kids. They were my friends. And I had my work friends (that I admittedly never saw outside of work, ever). And of course, there were my church friends. The ones who would invite me to women's events I was just too busy to attend.

But I had friends. At least, I thought I did. And then, at twenty-five years old, I lost a pregnancy.

And that's not the kind of thing you share with surface-level friends. Praise the Lord for an incredible husband and a mom and sister who were there for me, but those three were the extent of my support group.

I felt very alone, even though I was surrounded by women. At work, at church, and even at home. Kent was in seminary at the time, so we lived on campus. That means I was literally living next door to women who probably understood me better than anyone (Hello?! One of those women is my co-author!), but I had never worked to go deeper than "Hi" and "Bye."

I know they would have rallied for me. They would have been by my side, but I didn't feel right reaching out. I had chosen to spend my time making money instead of making friends, and I was finally forced to see the effects of my poor choices.

But money was a lot easier to make than friends. So you can see why I would do that, right?

I think working women are some of the toughest nuts to crack. We really are busy, so we actually do have to be protective of our time and who we share it with. But I had completely missed the point of my purpose.

No matter how passionate I am about the work, I am not here for a job. I'm here for people.

Why did I think I had to choose between a career and people? That's such a lie! And I really wish I could tell you that after my sad experience, I decided to change my ways and find real friends . . . but that wasn't the case. It took a few more years before I truly started building relationships.

And guess who was the one to drag me, kicking and screaming, into genuine friendship? My co-author, best friend, and SWHW partner, Michelle Myers.

When I tell you she did not let up on me, I mean that. She. Did. Not. Let. Up. Any of you have a friend like that? This woman called me, texted me, discipled me, encouraged me, invited me, affirmed me, spoke truth to me, sharpened me. She did it all. Total transparency: She drove me nuts (and she still does sometimes) but she also makes me better.

And look at us now. What would I have missed out on in my career if I had missed out first on that relationship?

Side note to those of you with all the friends, reading this chapter and wondering how any woman can survive life without them: If you don't struggle in this area, you can be somebody else's Michelle! Start praying now for that woman you can drag kicking and screaming into genuine friendship too!

I get it that you're busy. I totally understand that there will be seasons when you have more time for friends than maybe you do in the current season. But I was surrounded by women in my life who were also busy, and if I had just given them a chance, they probably would have welcomed my intermittent friendship with open arms because they were kind women who were in the same boat!

But I was so blinded by what I thought their expectation of me would be that I was too scared to even pursue the friendship.

Can we as women—working or not—all promise to let one another out of these unrealistic expectations for friendship? Unrealistic expectations can hold you back from friendship because you're scared you will let people down. And if you're one of those women holding others to expectations you've made up, if you stop looking outward, you might discover your expectations are more self-centered than you've allowed yourself to believe.

Friends are a gift. Treat them as such.

> Two are better than one,
>   because they have a good return for their labor:
> If either of them falls down,
>   one can help the other up.
> But pity anyone who falls
>   and has no one to help them up.
>
> Ecclesiastes 4:9–10 NIV

Mom or Not

And speaking of relationships, specifically the maternal ones, I want to clear something up. If you're a woman and a believer, chances are that whether you have biological children or not, you will someday take on (if you haven't already) a maternal role in someone else's life. Maybe a teenager from church you're discipling, a niece or nephew, or a young woman at work who has a strained relationship with her own family. So when we talk about motherhood here, it is not to exclude a woman without children, but to acknowledge, first of all, one of the greatest areas of contention in a working woman's life—being a mom who works—and second, to speak to our womanhood in a way much of culture is afraid to, as if it is offensive or degrading that a woman is seen as a nurturing or motherly individual. We will not participate in that narrative here because much of what the world sees as a weakness we see as a God-given strength, as do the people in your life who depend on you for love and nurturing. (We'll have to save this topic for another book.) But the bottom line is, when you read our stories of parenting, I pray that whether you are a mother in the traditional sense or in the spiritual sense, these stories will encourage and connect with you.

Where Really Matters

A few years ago, when we were at the height of teenage busyness, and it seemed one of my kids had something scheduled every day of the week, I met with my new marketing team. During the meeting, I was told how much I was lacking in consistently engaging on social media, and that if I was going to have a successful business (I owned a fitness studio at the time), I would have to be the "face"—which basically meant I'd have to be attached to my phone, building my platform.

At first, I felt badly, like I hadn't stewarded well what God had given me with this amazing studio. And then I got mad. It felt so unfair that the only way to win was by having yet another place, even if it was only on social media, that I had to show up every single day.

And then I got quiet. God quieted my emotions and assured me that if I put Him first and gave my family my best, He would sustain my business.

That was all I needed to hear.

Let me clarify: Social media wasn't the enemy here, so if you've been called to show up there consistently, do it and do it well. The issue was my heart. I had forgotten that His way doesn't always look like the world tells me it should.

So the next day, I woke up early and after some time with the Lord, I wrote this. And I've come back to read these words He gave me each and every time I start to feel pulled in the wrong direction.

» My family is my "ministry."
» My home is my "platform."
» My kids are my "followers."
» They're the "likes" I care about.
» They're my "warm market" I go above and beyond for.
» They're my long-term investment strategy and the best word-of-mouth advertisement I will ever get.

Pray it. Read it. Speak it. Believe it. #relationshipsfirst was God's idea.

People Are the Point

The story of Rebecca coming to be Isaac's wife is a favorite of mine. If you can take a minute to read it, head to Genesis 24 to do so, or you can follow my CliffsNotes version:

Abraham, the father of the nation of Israel, as well as Isaac's father, is close to death; Sarah, Isaac's mother, had already died, and Isaac was yet to marry. Abraham wanted to see that Isaac was married before he passed away, so he sent his servant with very specific instructions to find a wife for Isaac.

Enter lovely, faithful, kind Rebecca.

Here's the quick rundown:

- *Abraham's servant, a total stranger to Rebecca, shows up at the well where Rebecca is drawing water and asks her for water. Not only is he thirsty, but his camels are too.*
- *Rebecca kindly draws water for the man and his camels.*
- *He proceeds to ask if he and his entire entourage can spend the night at Rebecca's house, and she obliges.*
- *Rebecca finds out from her brother who this stranger is and that he has come a very long way to find a wife for the son of his master, Abraham, and that he thinks she is the one Isaac should marry.*
- *Rebecca agrees to go back with the servant, only to find out that he wants to leave immediately.*
- *She loads up all of her things, tells her family goodbye, and heads for a strange land to meet the strange man she's supposed to marry.*

This whole story is crazy! Rebecca's humbleness, courage, and instant obedience are mind-blowing. But get this: It all started with Rebecca making time for a stranger.

What if Rebecca had been too focused on herself or her tasks to stop and meet the needs of someone else? She would have missed this incredible opportunity!

Have you ever missed an opportunity to stop and serve someone because it was just one of those extra-busy days? You know, the kind of day when your schedule is really packed, and you're focused on a deadline, so you just keep to yourself?

Yeah, me too.

Oh Lord, help us to do better, and to really see the people and the needs that are around us.

Be Aware and Available

God is sovereign, so He is in full control. He can do what He wills with or without us, but if we want to be part of His plan, we must be like Rebecca: aware and available.

How aware are you?

Are you so distracted by what you have going on that you forget to look up and see the people God has placed in your path? I promise you they're not there by accident. You don't know what that "drink of water" can lead to!

How available are you?

Do you find yourself avoiding people you know need or desire time with you because you just don't have the margin?

If people are the point (and they are!), then our schedules should reflect that. Creating margin for people isn't just a scheduling tip, it's a biblical command.

And ultimately, serving others serves Christ.

> Then the King will say to those on his right, "Come, you who are blessed by my Father; take your inheritance, the kingdom prepared for you since the creation of the world. For I was hungry and you gave me something to eat, I was thirsty and you gave me something to drink, I was a stranger and you invited me in, I needed clothes and you clothed me, I was sick and you looked after me, I was in prison and you came to visit me."
>
> Then the righteous will answer him, "Lord, when did we see you hungry and feed you, or thirsty and give you something to

> drink? When did we see you a stranger and invite you in, or needing clothes and clothe you? When did we see you sick or in prison and go to visit you?"
>
> The King will reply, **"Truly I tell you, whatever you did for one of the least of these brothers and sisters of mine, you did for me."**
>
> Matthew 25:34–40 NIV, emphasis added

Getting personal and meeting needs is not something we can dismiss, delegate, or deflect. It's not merely the job of an organization, but a personal responsibility for each of us. And not just any responsibility, but one that may result in one of His biggest blessings on your earthly life.

Relationships will always matter most. Always.

A Prayer to Prioritize Relationships over Achievements

Father, make me more like You,
especially in the way You love people.
I know and rely on Your love, God,
Make me one who abides in You, so I abide in love.[6]

Help me see souls—not just what my eyes see.
Help me to love others for who You've made them to be
and not for what they can do for me.
Help me to love people genuinely,
And to remember that love is an action, not merely a feeling.

Help me to see everyone as my equal.
To remember that we were created in Your image,[7]
And that the reason Jesus died was for us,
For every single one of us.[8]

Forgive me for holding on to relational hurt from my past.
Do not allow me to pursue past hurt more than new relationships.
Help me to forgive and pursue relationships without hesitation.
Forgive me and rid me of bitterness, resentment, and jealousy.
Delete my ill feelings for the difficult people in my life,
and replace those feelings with Your love.

6. 1 John 4:16.
7. Genesis 1:27.
8. 2 Corinthians 5:15.

And give me grace, God,
So much of your supernatural grace,
So that I can forgive and love others, despite their behavior,
Just as you have forgiven and loved me despite mine.[9]
Give others grace for me, so that they can receive love from me,
Even if I have not been perfect in loving them.

Open my eyes to the people You have placed in my life
That I can love as You have loved me.[10]
Give me opportunities to go deeper,
And use our relationships to bring glory to Yourself.

God, I surrender my daily schedule to You.
I promise to leave margin for Your children.
Help me to do what I need to in my own life to open up more space
So that I can live in community,[11]
Love my neighbor,[12]
And spur on my brothers and sisters the way You've called me to.[13]

Amen.

9. Romans 5:8.
10. John 15:12.
11. Hebrews 10:25.
12. Mark 12:31.
13. Hebrews 10:24.

8

Love

Skill

Michelle

> ***Culture says***: Measure your work by your level of skill.
>
> ***God says***: Measure your work by the level of My love you show through it.

A few years ago, James surprised me by getting us tickets to a Cubs game when we had a work trip near Chicago. When we took our seats, I couldn't help but notice the usher in front of us. Probably not far from retirement age, he had a great smile, a contagious laugh, and tons of energy. But not only that, he worked hard. From helping people find their seat to waving down concession workers to being the loudest fan in the stadium, he was never idle.

Every inning, multiple people came up to him. Selfies, handshakes, high fives—it seemed like everyone at the game knew him! Curiosity got the best of me, so when I realized we were seated next to season ticket holders, I asked them, "Who is he? Was he a player or is he a celebrity I just don't recognize?"

They laughed. "Around here, he's a celebrity for sure. He has been working in this section for twenty years, and he's the best. I've never seen him have a bad day."

His job was far from glamorous. It was hot, everyone had a seat in our section but him, and his work didn't slow down the entire game. But the love he had, probably not so much for the job itself, but for the people he came in contact with, was obvious, even for me at first glance.

Real question: When you work, what is most obviously on display, love or skill?

Even the secular world notes that skill will only get you so far. (Run a quick Google search for "hire character, train skill" and see how many sources pop up!) No matter how skilled you may be, if you have a reputation of a bad attitude or being difficult to work with, eventually it will catch up with you. Anyone who has ever hired based on skill alone can testify: Most any skill can be learned. Character is not only much harder to learn, but it's much more important.

And while experience has taught the world this is true, love and skill being intertwined is a biblical principle.

Known by Our Love

You've probably heard 1 Corinthians 13 ("Love is patient, love is kind . . .") shared at nearly every wedding you've attended. Coined "The Love Chapter," it often serves as the standard to which we are held in loving one another.

And it's a good standard to use. Your marriage will certainly thrive if you put this into practice. But the original audience was not at a wedding, and the context of the chapter isn't about marriage; it's about how we are to use the gifts God gives us.

Paul's letters were not written in chapters and verses (those were added later to make referencing easier), so rather than reading this passage as an isolated discourse on love, we must read it as Paul's continuation of a discussion of spiritual gifts that starts in 1 Corinthians 12 and continues into Chapter 14.

Here's what was happening in the Corinthian church: Instead of serving their intended purpose of strengthening and unifying the church, spiritual gifts were dividing it. Hierarchies developed, depending on an individual's spiritual gift, creating competition and comparison—the enemies of unity. What was happening then still happens today. We misunderstand, and subsequently misuse, spiritual gifts. Instead of being used to serve God and others, gifts are used to inflate our own egos or they go unused by immature recipients. And as our world becomes increasingly autonomous, layers of comparison and competition still keep the church divided instead of functioning as a body.

Paul starts by setting the church at Corinth straight about what spiritual gifts are, and then he moves on to make sure they know how to use them: with love. According to Paul, saying the right words without love reduces them to noise that distracts, and doing the right actions without love robs both you and the gift of all purpose and effectiveness.[1]

Let those words sink in. Without love, our gifts are merely distractions, purposeless and ineffective. Love makes the difference in whether our gifts are useful to God, not our level of skill. I'm certainly not against skill, but remember: Jesus said we would be identifiable as His by our love[2]—not because we're the best.

Conversations about love and skill should not be isolated. So let's look at what God says about spiritual gifts and the

1. 1 Corinthians 13:1–3.
2. John 13:35.

love that must accompany them to make what He has given us eternally beneficial.

Spiritual Gifts 101

Here's a quick summary of Paul's insight into spiritual gifts—straight from 1 Corinthians 12.[3]

- *Every spiritual gift is given by God (vv. 4–7).*
- *Everyone receives a spiritual gift from God (v. 7).*
- *Everyone does not receive the same gift (v. 4).*
- *God allows for gifts to be used in different ways (v. 5).*
- *God, who gives the gift, determines the gift's importance, not the gift itself (vv. 4–7).*
- *Your spiritual gift should be used to serve and strengthen others (v. 7).*
- *God empowers you to use the gifts He gives you (v. 11).*
- *No spiritual gift is more important than another (vv. 15–17).*
- *All spiritual gifts are needed (v. 17).*
- *God put you where you are to use the gift He gave you (v. 18).*
- *Our spiritual gifts are meant to unify us (vv. 20, 25).*
- *Together, we display Jesus to the world (v. 27).*

We probably wouldn't disagree on any of the above, regardless of how well we live it out. But there are two more things I think culture twists most often:

Discontentment Is Pride

Culture Twist #1: Selfishness is easy to identify when we use our gifts just so we can take credit for it. But there's a selfishness

3. For more on spiritual gifts, see Romans 12, 1 Peter 4, and Ephesians 4.

that often flies under the radar that can be just as deadly: discontentment with what God has given us.

Typically, if we refuse to use the gift we have and insist on a different one, we don't really desire to use the gift for God; we merely desire the earthly reward we believe comes with it. God gives us gifts to use for His glory and to serve one another.[4] Believing God did not give us a gift worth using is selfishness.

So yes, guard against pride that presents itself as arrogance. But we must also recognize that discontentment is still pride, just in a less obvious form. God is what satisfies you, not the gift He gives. Waiting on a particular gift to satisfy you is seeking satisfaction outside of God himself . . . which means you will never be satisfied.

And culture is relentless in prioritizing what is shiny, but not what is actually valuable. As believers, what we have to remember is that this world is not where my story or your story ends, but it's where our stories begin.

Jobs you get or don't get.

Stuff you accumulate or can't afford.

Applause or silence.

Fame or obscurity.

If my life is a vapor[5] and I'm supposed to function as a stranger[6] just passing through, I don't want to waste the brief time God has given me here dwelling on an earthly reward that may or may not come when I can be confident of what He has promised me is with Him in heaven.[7]

Eternity can be an overwhelming concept if we allow ourselves to get consumed with what we do not know. I will never claim to be an expert, but I am confident in this: I want to live

4. 1 Peter 4:10.
5. James 4:14.
6. 1 Peter 2:11.
7. John 14:1–3.

like earth is an introduction to my eternal life—not as if eternity is merely the conclusion to my earthly life.

Unity > Unique

Culture Twist #2: You do not lose your uniqueness when you come to Christ. Just as Paul used the analogy of the body parts being different in function but equal in importance, each of us has a unique God-given story, purpose, and placement. But in Christ, your uniqueness yields to unity. You are still unique, but prioritizing uniqueness makes it about you, and prioritizing unity makes it about the kingdom.

Being "better together" is not a corny slogan created by the world, but the intentional design of our loving Father. And it's not just coming together in gifts, but in love. Without love, as Paul writes, our gifts profit nothing.[8]

When Jesus took every law and condensed it to loving God and loving others,[9] He made the law easier to remember, but more challenging to live. And just as love raised the standard of the law, love raises the standard for our skill as well. We are not merely called to use the skill God gave us, but to use our skill with love as God defines it:

Patient. Kind. Free of envy, boasting, and pride. Honoring others. Not self-seeking, not easily angered, and keeping no record of wrongs. Refusing to delight in evil, but rejoicing in the truth. Protecting, trusting, hoping, and persevering . . . always.[10]

Skill may fail, but this kind of love will not.[11] So let's talk practically of what it looks like to raise our skill to His standard of love.

8. 1 Corinthians 13:2–3.
9. Matthew 22:36–40.
10. 1 Corinthians 13:4–7.
11. 1 Corinthians 13:8.

Love Is Patient: Trust God's Timing

We truly live in a microwave world where so much is available to us instantly that we dread waiting. But God doesn't waste anything—waiting included.

When I think about someone who had to wait, my mind jumps to Joseph. As a young boy, having been gifted to interpret dreams, Joseph dreamed that one day he would rule over all of his family. For his brothers, already jealous because Joseph was their father's favorite, his dream was the last straw. His brothers sold him into slavery, and then lied to their father, saying he had been killed by a wild animal.[12]

Joseph was purchased by a powerful man named Potiphar. Eventually, Joseph won Potiphar's favor, and Potiphar put Joseph in charge of everything he owned. Unfortunately, Joseph also caught the attention of Potiphar's wife. After Joseph rejected her repeated sexual advances, she accused Joseph of attempting to rape her, so he was thrown into prison over her false accusation.[13]

So much for the dream God had given him, right?

Except that isn't the end of Joseph's story. In prison, the chief jailer put Joseph in charge over all the prisoners. Two prisoners under his care, the king's cupbearer and baker, both had dreams they couldn't understand, so Joseph used his God-given gift and interpreted their dreams for them.[14]

Joseph's only request was that the cupbearer remember him when he was released . . . but the cupbearer didn't remember to tell Pharaoh about Joseph until two years later, when Pharaoh is in need of someone to interpret his troubling dream.[15]

12. Genesis 37.
13. Genesis 39.
14. Genesis 39:21–22; Genesis 40.
15. Genesis 40:14; Genesis 41.

Joseph's interpretation of Pharaoh's dream allows Egypt to prepare for a seven-year famine. In gratitude, Pharaoh makes Joseph second in command over all of Egypt. (And eventually, his brothers do bow down to him, and Scripture records a beautiful moment of forgiveness and restoration.[16])

Don't miss this: Repeatedly throughout Joseph's story, we read that "the Lord was with" Joseph.[17]

Thirteen years passed between Joseph's being sold by his brothers and his coming into power in Egypt. Joseph served faithfully and patiently as God used slavery and prison as his training ground for the palace.

Patience is found in God's presence, not in your circumstances. So if you find yourself wondering how God could ever use where you are right now, fight the urge to rush God's timing and instead rush into God's presence. What the world sees as a detour, God can use as preparation. Stay close to Him and remain patient.

So let me talk for a minute to those of you who don't have your dream job. You work out of provision and necessity. Although your job isn't what you thought you'd be doing, and you don't love it, be faithful where you are anyway. Waiting on God's timing doesn't mean His work in your life comes to a stop.

The work Joseph did in prison wouldn't make anyone's goal list, but he still found a way to be faithful in using what God had given him even in the obscurest of places. Jesus said, "The harvest is plentiful" (aka the work is ready!) "but the workers are few."[18] You can be His worker right where you are—no waiting and no new assignment required. Only a new perspective.

16. Genesis 42:6; Genesis 45.
17. Genesis 39:2, 3, 21, 23.
18. Matthew 9:37 NIV.

Love Is Kind: See People for Who They Are, Not What They Do

People need to know that you care about them far more than you care about the task they do. Workers who are viewed as tasks will feel used, not loved. Undervalued people don't work hard, and people typically won't stay where they feel used.

The more important the mission is, the easier it is to stop prioritizing people. Sounds crazy, but it's true: The more purpose that exists in the tasks themselves, the more likely you are to see the tasks being done and not the people who are doing them. (Ministry leaders, I am especially talking to us on this one!)

But no one had a more important mission than Jesus, and He never stopped seeing people and caring for them, despite what He was doing or what they were doing.

- *The woman at the well had been through multiple husbands and was currently living with a man who wasn't her husband. Jesus saw her, showed kindness, and her radical testimony brought salvation to many Samaritans.*[19]
- *Zacchaeus was a rich tax collector, but after Jesus' kindness, he gave half of his possessions to the poor and agreed to give back four times as much to anyone he had cheated in the past.*[20]
- *Even Judas. Have you ever noticed how Jesus greets him when Judas betrays Jesus with a kiss on the night of His arrest? Instead of calling him traitor, betrayer, or liar (all of which would have been true), Jesus looked at Judas, not his action, and simply said, "Friend, do what you came to do."*[21] *For our Savior, the cross, which was one of*

19. John 4:1–42.
20. Luke 19:1–10.
21. Matthew 26:50.

> *the cruelest ways to die, was an intentional act of love far more than a plotted act of violence—right from the moment when he looked His betrayer in the face and called him "friend."*

Create evidence that you love people for who they are—loved children of God—not for what they may or may not be doing.

The shy woman in the office who everyone thinks is stuck up? Smile, look her in the eyes, and ask her a question to get to know her better instead of just rushing past her desk. Kindness is a better approach to helping someone open up than ignoring them.

The impossible-to-please boss who barks orders? Don't stoop to her level. Point out the good in her—directly to her and to others. Stay grateful. Do your best work. Pray for God to open doors for you to bless her beyond merely doing your job, and when He does, run through them.

The scattered assistant who has to do things twice because she doesn't get them right the first time? Instead of rolling your eyes and being frustrated that she can't figure it out, take time to train her and answer her questions. Go out of your way to make it fun and intentional, and watch to see a case study of how loved people do better work unfold before you.

And if you're the leader? Be intentional not to attach your kindness to performance. Be kind when they do a great job, and be kind when it's mediocre at best. It doesn't mean that you can't address matters when something needs to improve, but there's a way to be clear in your expectations while still being kind.

One more note for leaders: Beyond simply reacting kindly, be proactive in showing kindness. My friend, Dani, excitedly texted me on a random 70-degree day in February because her boss gave her the day off to enjoy the sunshine. As you can imagine, she felt over-the-top valued! Creativity shouldn't be reserved just for what we produce. Be creative in how you care for others.

Love Does Not Envy: Celebrate + Support

Many adolescent struggles don't go away. As we get older, we simply rename them to make ourselves feel better. Envy and jealousy, for example, sound like struggles we should grow out of, which is why we created a glamourized, socially accepted version we call "comparison."

In his last letter, Paul told Timothy to "flee youthful passions and pursue righteousness, faith, love, and peace, along with those who call on the Lord from a pure heart."[22] Paul is reminding Timothy that growing spiritually is the only way to actually mature. Otherwise, we just get older.

If we desire to mature, we must be willing to confront our sin instead of seeking our own comfort. It's not okay to believe that struggling with comparison is not a big deal just because everyone else struggles too. We can't refuse to take ownership while hastily blaming the internet. Mature people don't do immature things.

Comparison is still a struggle in adulthood when we do not make efforts to get rid of the envy in our hearts. And envy is a big deal! Envy creates division among you and another child of God, and envy steals from our kingdom energy. When you allow yourself to get so consumed watching someone else live their life, you miss living the life God gave you.

Keep in mind: Envy in the heart sometimes manifests as criticism. If you don't feel that you're overly jealous of someone,

22. 2 Timothy 2:22.

examine who you take the time to tear down. It might not merely be a critical spirit speaking, but envy.

What you spend most of your time doing is who you are, which is why we must stay away from things that don't matter. You'll either be a busybody or busy on mission. You can't be both.

Love doesn't stop at simply refusing to envy. Love actively celebrates and supports. Make efforts to champion those the world would say are your competition.

Here's a quick evaluation to see how often you support and celebrate others:

- *When something good happens to a friend, do they share it with you personally? If you usually hear about good news from friends on social media and not personally, you might not be known for celebrating others well.*
- *Do people know they can come to you if they need help? If no one comes to you for help, others may not think they can count on you for support.*
- *Are you friends with anyone the world would see as your competition? If sharing a business market automatically makes you regard someone as an enemy, there's definitely room for growth.*
- *Do others speak up in the meetings you lead? If they do, you've created a culture of collaboration where the best idea wins. If you're the only one with ideas, it might not be your team's fault. If your idea always wins, take ownership for their silence and show them you value their contribution by going with their ideas whenever possible.*
- *Do you invest in others—even when there's nothing in it for you personally or when it's completely unrelated to work? You will encounter a lot more people you can support than you can hire and people you encounter through your job*

have a lot more to offer this world beyond being your co-worker or your customer. Be as generous as you can to make personal interactions a personal investment.

Bonus challenge: Brainstorm a way to support and celebrate your biggest competition right now. Write it down, then do it. You might be surprised by the space that showing her love frees up in your heart.

Love Does Not Boast + Is Not Proud: Stay Teachable

The saying, "If you are the smartest person in the room, you're in the wrong room" is shared so often that it's been attributed to too many people to know who actually said it first. And while I certainly don't disagree that we should surround ourselves with people who are smarter than we are, as believers, I also don't think that we should be so prideful as to believe a room exists where we're incapable of learning. What good can come from boasting that you're ready for a new room? Boasting keeps you focused on what you've already done instead of what's left to be done. Boasting is a huge distraction.

Some of my greatest teachers are currently ten, seven, and five years old—God uses my kids to teach me things all the time. So maybe the saying should go: If you are typically the smartest person in the room, humility may be able to teach you more than a new room ever could.

Here are some ways you can pursue humility while using your gifts:

- *Apologize and be willing to admit your mistakes.*
- *Ask questions and learn from others.*
- *Ask for help.*
- *Stay approachable.*

- *Have an honest close circle. Honesty will always take you further than flattery.*

Love Does Not Dishonor Others: Make the Effort to Honor

Dishonoring others can be done quickly and without much thought. In settings of using our gifts, dishonoring others usually takes these forms:

- *Gossip*
- *Developing cliques and hierarchies*
- *Sarcasm (insults we disguise as comedy)*

Honoring others, conversely, requires our intentionality, not merely our reactions. So to honor others, we should:

- *Deal with problems privately and individually.*
- *Make efforts toward unity and inclusion.*
- *Encourage others privately, publicly, and often.*

Keep in mind that apathy results in dishonor. Encouragement that goes unspoken or gratitude that is unexpressed are just thoughts. Make the effort to honor.

Love Is Not Self-Seeking: Separate Self from Ambition

Quick quiz:

- *Is it difficult for you to be happy when someone else succeeds?*
- *Is it tough for you to turn your brain off, rest, or slow down?*
- *Do you struggle to listen to others?*

- *Do you try to do God's work without God?*
- *Do you frequently dream of getting your "big break"?*
- *Do you often pursue something new after watching someone have success?*
- *Do you equate your purpose in life with your achievements?*

Count up your yes answers and that will give you an idea of how much self is still included in your skill. There's a reason why there's so much caution against selfish ambition in Scripture. But it's self that takes us in the wrong direction—not ambition.

Look at how much wisdom is packed into these words from Paul:

> I make it my ambition to preach the gospel, not where Christ has already been named, lest I build on someone else's foundation.
>
> Romans 15:20

First and foremost, kingdom ambition is about the Gospel and spreading it where Christ is not known. The mark of kingdom ambition is when the mission blazes a new trail for the Lord, not simply going down the path of another successful Christian.

Could God call you to a similar assignment another believer has? Absolutely, He can. It's not about what you're doing, but Whom you're following. Are you following God and where He is taking you because of what's in it for Him? Or are you simply following a person because of what you think may be in it for you?

Let the potential for the Gospel, not the potential for self, determine your direction. Loving God and loving others will absolutely require your ambition. So stay ambitious—just refuse to let your ambition be centered in self.

Love Is Not Easily Angered: Overlook Most Offenses

We live in a world that is easily offended. And in today's world, where we can argue instantly behind screens with brave thumbs, we often need to be reminded of the biblical wisdom that "it is to one's glory to overlook an offense."[23]

Here's the problem: No offense feels minor in the moment. Rudeness from a stranger, when your boss goes on a power trip, when a co-worker is hypercritical—all offenses feel major. But when we allow ourselves to focus on minor things, major things are missed.

For example, when Paul writes the church at Philippi, he acknowledges that while he is in prison, some are preaching the Gospel out of envy and selfish ambition rather than from pure motives.

And rather than calling them out, getting angry, or allowing himself to become bitter because they were freely preaching the same message that put him in prison, what does Paul do? He rejoices.[24] Instead of getting worked up over why the Gospel was being preached, Paul chooses to simply rejoice that the Gospel was being preached.

If we stop and think about it, we all can probably identify someone who has offended us. It's not that the offense wasn't real or that the offense was right. But people will offend you, so if you plan to keep working with people, you will save yourself from so much frustration if you will resolve to get good at overlooking offenses.

Total honesty: Seeking justice comes much more naturally to me than giving grace. So here's the rule I've made for myself: If in five years it won't matter, it's not worth even five minutes of my attention now.

23. Proverbs 19:11 NIV.
24. Philippians 1:15–18

Overlook most offenses so you have maximum time to do what matters.

Love Keeps No Record of Wrongs: Stop Keeping Score

Sometimes, I wonder how many great ideas have gone unspoken due to fear of being wrong. I wonder how many solutions that would have worked have gone unpursued simply over the fear of making a mistake.

There is not a single organization that will thrive when mistakes are magnified and harped on rather than expected and learned through. People are not perfect, so organizations that expect perfection will remain in disappointment.

Share the wins and share the mistakes. Learn together. Accept blame before you place blame. Instead of allowing past mistakes to hold you back, view them as learning experiences so when you try again, you're better prepared.

In a culture of fear, people hide mistakes, cut corners, do the bare minimum, and will not take initiative unless asked. Conversations are avoided, feelings are assumed, questions go unasked, and distance grows while buy-in plummets.

In a culture of love, however, people aren't afraid to ask for help, go the extra mile, jump in to assist with someone else's responsibility, or take a calculated risk that just might work. Communication is open, problems get resolved, and loyalty grows along with ownership.

Think about Peter. Jesus says about him, "upon this rock, I will build My church."[25] But then Peter denies Jesus three times on the night before He is crucified.[26] Peter is devastated. Feeling he had messed up beyond measure, days later, his simple

25. Matthew 16:18 NASB.
26. Luke 22:54–62.

statement "I am going fishing"[27] was basically his way of saying, "I'm going back to my old life."

But guess what? Jesus forgives Peter and reaffirms his calling by asking him three times, "Do you love me?" And after Peter replied "yes" each time, Jesus followed Peter's professed love for Him with a charge: Feed my lambs, tend my sheep, and feed my sheep.[28]

Be the kind of person who allows others to make mistakes and grow through them. God will put Peters in your path—and you can be the difference between shame taking them back to their old life or lovingly reaffirming who God made them to be.

Love Does Not Delight in Evil but Rejoices with Truth

We live in a world where many people rejoice over the failures of others as much as they enjoy their own success. You will have many opportunities throughout your career to delight in evil. Stand firm.

When a conniving co-worker announces she and her husband are getting a divorce? Don't waste a single second being satisfied in her pain. In compassion, pray for her family.

When someone you discerned had impure motives experiences public failure? Refuse to rejoice. Pray for her restoration.

Reserve rejoicing for truth—keeping in mind that not all truth is easy to say or to receive, but that truth always helps more than it hurts—especially when truth is not separated from love, realizing that God is both love[29] and truth.[30]

I always come back to this reminder from Warren Wiersbe that "truth without love is brutality and love without truth is hypocrisy."[1]

27. John 21:3.
28. John 21:15–17.
29. 1 John 4:8.
30. John 14:6.

Constantly come back to truth and only rejoice in it.

Love Always Protects, Trusts, Hopes, Perseveres: Quit Quitting

Love that comes from God isn't fragile. We serve a God who conquered the grave, and yet we give up over obstacles that are far less intimidating. We know how this world ends. Jesus wins! So any time we allow ourselves to fight the wrong battles, get discouraged over minor issues, or become distracted by a defeated enemy, we've simply lost focus on what matters most.

Remember the real battle, and quit quitting over lesser things. Live and love in a way that protects, trusts, hopes, and perseveres.

What if we all had this reminder where we could see it every day?

» a reminder to use my skill with love «

__________ [YOUR NAME] is patient and kind. __________ [YOUR NAME] does not envy or boast. __________ [YOUR NAME] is not arrogant or rude. __________ [YOUR NAME] does not insist on her own way. __________ [YOUR NAME] is not irritable or resentful. __________ [YOUR NAME] does not rejoice in wrong doing, but rejoices with the truth. __________ [YOUR NAME] bears all things, believes all things, hopes all things, endures all things.

-adapted from 1 corinthians 13:4-7

Fill in the blanks with your name and read it aloud. (True story: The first time I did this exercise, I could barely choke out the words, "Michelle is patient.") But the truth is that if we want to live and work His way, it has to move beyond mere desire. It must be demonstrated. And there's no better guide for how it should be done than the verses above.

Love Never Fails

Paul ends his discussion on love with this thought:

> And now these three remain: faith, hope and love. But the greatest of these is love.
>
> 1 Corinthians 13:13 NIV

Faith is our foundation. Everything comes back to responding to who God is and what God has done.

Hope is our motivation. Because of Jesus, our perspective can stay set on things above.[31]

Love is movement. It's how we put faith and hope into action.

No matter where you are and no matter what gift you have been given, you have the capacity to increase your influence and impact by measuring your skill not by the task or talent, but by the amount of love that goes with it.

31. Colossians 3:2.

A Prayer to Measure Skill by Love

Father, You are the giver of every skill I have.
Forgive me when I've allowed Your gift
To inflate my own ego or importance
Or immaturely go unused as if Your gifts were solely
for my benefit.

Help me desire You, God, not Your gifts.
And make me grateful for the gifts You've given to others.
Rather than the measurements the world uses,
Help me to measure my gifts with the love that goes
with them.

Lord, make me patient.
I trust Your timing.
When I'm tempted to rush Your timing,
Remind me to rush into Your presence instead.
You are all I need.

Lord, make me kind.
Help me see others for who You made them to be,
Not simply how they're behaving in the moment.
Give me opportunities to show Your kindness to them,
Even when it's not deserved.
I praise You for dealing kindly with me.

Lord, free me from envy.
Do not let me dismiss envy as comparison,
But help me confront my sin rather than coddle my
own comfort.
Show me ways I can serve those the world says are my
competition,
And may my actions prove I see others as allies and not
enemies.

Lord, make me teachable.
Give me the humility to admit when I'm wrong.
Do not let me fall for flattery,
Or become distracted by boasting.
Keep teaching me, Lord, and use Your children to teach me.

Lord, keep my actions far from dishonor.
Do not let gossip or hierarchies have a grip on me,
But put unity and inclusion constantly on my heart.
Give me opportunities to encourage and honor others
To stir them up to love and good works.[32]

Lord, remove every inch of self from my ambition.
Help me create kingdom wins where Christ is not known.
Determine my direction where there is potential for the Gospel,
Forgetting potential for self.
Make every effort that I pursue solely for my own gain a failure,
Until I turn back to pursue kingdom success alone.

Lord, help me overlook most offenses,
So I have the maximum time to pursue what matters.
Lord, I am so undeserving of the grace You freely give me.
Help me to forgive others,
To the same measure I have been forgiven.[33]

Lord, help me stop keeping score.
Help me accept the blame before I place blame on others.
When others around me make mistakes,
Help me detour shame from holding them back

32. Hebrews 10:24.
33. Matthew 6:14–15.

by lovingly reaffirming who You made them to be.

Lord, thrill my soul with Your truth,
And the endurance to quit quitting over things
that pale in comparison to You.
Keep me holding fast to You,
the Love that never fails.

Amen.

9

Listen

Be Heard

Somer

This world is loud, so it's easy to assume that the only way to get attention is by being louder. Why do you think people will say and do the most ridiculous, dangerous, or humiliating things on the internet just to go viral?

To fulfill a deep desire to be seen and heard.

God knows us so well though. He knew this desire could be a problem, so He addressed it. A lot.[1]

You've heard the saying, "God gave us two ears and one mouth because we're supposed to listen twice as much as we speak." It's cute, right?

But it's also truer than we probably even know.

1. Proverbs 18:13, Proverbs 19:27, James 1:19, Luke 11:28, Romans 10:17, Matthew 18:15, Jeremiah 33:3.

If you're a talker, or a fixer, or a debater, or just someone who finds silence hard, you'll want to prepare to get a little uncomfortable, but I promise it will be worth it. Because prioritizing listening isn't just a polite behavior, or a leadership strategy, it's a God-honoring command that we hear about all through Scripture.

A Listening Leader

In Paul's first letter to Thessalonica, he reassures them that what he and Timothy had taught them about the Gospel was true.[2] And Paul reminds them their visit and work in Thessalonica was not for any gain of their own, but strictly because it was what God asked them to do. As you read, you can sense how very much Paul desired to keep their trust.

But then, Paul gives us the most beautiful picture of how a leader should handle the people he or she serves:

> But we were gentle among you, like a nursing mother taking care of her own children. So, being affectionately desirous of you, we were ready to share with you not only the gospel of God but also our own selves, because you had become very dear to us.
>
> 1 Thessalonians 2:7–8

Three powerful lessons we can take from these two short verses:

"Like a nursing mother": The intimate example he uses of a nursing mother says it all. Paul, the hot-tempered loud guy, had figured out that one of the best ways to serve people was to be gentle with them.

"Being affectionately desirous": This mission was not a to-do he needed to check off before moving on to his next location. This was a calling he cared deeply about, involving people for

2. 1 Thessalonians 2.

whom he had developed affection. Paul didn't just desire to get the message out, but he desired this message to actually be received by those who heard it. (It's entirely possible for someone to hear you without receiving what you say.)

"Ready to share . . . our own selves": Paul knew that it would take more than his words to move them to action, so he offered himself. Plainly put? Paul really got to know these people. And how do you get to know someone? By listening.

You can't get to know someone if you're the only one talking. It's impossible to love and serve people well if we neglect to hear them. Their loves, their fears, their dreams, their desires—all of that must be important to us!

A Listening Pastor

I grew up in a family of strong, charismatic, manly men: mostly hunters, pastors, law enforcement officers, and cowboys. Many of them had dynamic personalities they used to serve the Lord well. Christmas morning with my side of the family was loud, chaotic, and so much fun. I'm so thankful for their example in my life.

But as we girls so often do when we're looking for "the one," I was drawn to the opposite of what I'd always known. Enter Kent Phoebus.

He was the most laid-back, chill human I had ever known. A surfer, a drummer, a bit of an artist, incredibly kind, and so gentle. He also loved the Lord like I'd never seen a young man love Him. I was immediately interested.

It's impossible to love and serve people well if we neglect to hear them.

I remember the first time he asked me to pray with him at the end of a date and I was totally freaked out. (That shows you my spiritual maturity at the time.) A few months into our engagement, we were serving at a youth conference, and he felt God leading him to ministry. I saw how serious he was in that moment, and I knew there was no questioning this calling. He was sure.

Embarrassingly, I remember having instant doubts. Not about our relationship, but about his actually being a pastor. He just didn't look the part to me. Remember, Kent was quiet and laid-back. He didn't even like to order in the drive-through, so I would yell across him.

So how would this quiet guy become the booming voice on a stage, or a confident leader in a church meeting, or the one to meet a grieving family at the hospital? As a pastor's daughter, I knew the role of ministry well (or so I thought!), and I just wasn't convinced.

Fast-forward twenty-one years and oh my, how wrong I was.

Kent has served so well throughout his ministry. Turns out, lighting up a stage is a very small percentage of what good pastors or leaders actually do. And those church meetings? They run best when there are peacemakers in leadership. Also, a grieving family in the midst of a tragedy doesn't really need you to talk. They just need you to be there with them.

And I have watched him just be there so many times for so many people.

Kent taught me that before we lead, we have to listen. Like, really listen.

What if we didn't count on our charisma, or any of our gifts for that matter, to serve God? What if we just counted on Him? Fully expecting Him to pull out of us the right gifts at the right times to meet people right where they are?

God used Kent's quiet gift of gentleness to help him lead people. A gift that I didn't think fit the description of a pastor, or really any leader in my mind. But I quickly learned that the reason he was able to be so gentle and quiet was because he relied so heavily on God's ability to be heard.

Talk about countercultural! You want to look drastically different from the world? Try leading quietly.

A Listening Talker

I'm sure there are some very loud personalities reading this right now thinking, But what about me? I'm just really excited; I don't mean to be so loud. Do I have to change?

I wish I could come hug you and reassure you that it's absolutely okay to be loud and opinionated, and dare I say, a bit bossy, if that's the way God made you! It's just that people like us (yes, I'm one of you—I guess that's why Kent and I work so well together) have to be very, very careful not to begin enjoying the sound of our own voice more than we enjoy the sound of what God has to say.

Those of us who are gifted with words should absolutely use them for the glory of God. The book you're reading right now contains a lot of words that God has asked us to share with you, so we're obviously all for using our words and our voices to proclaim the Gospel.

If you feel you've been gifted with words, whether to teach or speak or write, absolutely do it! But make it your daily habit to open your Bible before you open your mouth, and surround yourself with solid godly voices you can listen to before you speak.

A Listening Mom

I am the mother of two female young adults. Both smart, both creative, and both currently in the midst of making big life decisions. FYI, parents of little ones, parenting doesn't get easier as your kids get older. It just grows into a different kind of hard.

But an encouraging and deeply rewarding kind of hard, if that makes sense?

Instead of potty training and tantrums, Kent and I are up to our eyeballs in deep theological and cultural questions as our daughters try to navigate their way through the political dumpster fires and make sense of this broken world. As challenging as it is, I wouldn't trade these conversations for the world.

Can I tell you the greatest lesson I've learned in having conversations with my kids? Our best and most productive talks are the ones where I listen more than I speak.

I know that may be hard because you feel like it's your responsibility to teach them everything they need to know in the short eighteen years you have them under your roof, but hear me: It's worth the effort it takes to restrain your mouth and limit your lectures.

Teachable moments aren't only accomplished with words.

Here's the truth—and honestly, this applies beyond parenting too—if every conversation turns into a lecture, that sweet kiddo of yours is going to eventually avoid talking to you all together.

Andy Stanley said this in a room of leaders, but it's also true for parents (and if you're a parent, you're a leader):

"Leaders who refuse to listen will eventually be surrounded by people who have nothing significant to say."[1]

One time I saw this play out in my own life was when my oldest daughter was a junior in high school and there was a big music festival she wanted to attend taking place near where we live. Our family loves music. Some families go to amusement parks or museums. We go to concerts. It's our thing.

My concern with this particular concert, though, was the huge crowd full of people making terrible decisions for three straight days, combined with her young age. Part of me (most of me, actually) just wanted to say no. I had plenty of reasons I could have listed.

But I also knew this: Just one, short year later, she would be moving into adulthood with the freedom to make these kinds of decisions entirely on her own.

So we decided the wisest thing for our kid would be to let her practice. And although it was super hard, Kent and I decided to let her make this decision on her own, knowing full well that we would have to live with whatever choice she made.

We skipped the lecture completely, briefly shared our opinion, and then told her we trusted her and that it was up to her; we said we would pray for her as she decided what to do.

And boy, did we pray! And we asked close friends who loved her to pray too. Either way, whatever decision she came to, we just wanted her to experience God's voice. That was the lesson here. And she did!

Ultimately, she decided not to go. Funny enough, that one experience made her feel so understood and trusted that at an age when a lot of us parents begin to feel distant from our teenagers, we found her coming back to us to seek our counsel more and more.

The greatest part of this whole experience, though, was that in listening to her, we were able to encourage her to listen to the Holy Spirit. It showed all of us that she didn't need to "borrow" Him from her mom's and dad's lives because as a believer, she had access to Him directly.

We knew He loved her, and she loved Him, which meant all we had to do was pray and trust them both.

That truth taught us a lot about parenting, but also about how important it is in any relationship, especially the ones where we lead, to pray for people and encourage them to seek the Holy Spirit more than our opinions, or anyone else's for that matter.

Kent and I have since made James 1:19 our parenting anthem:

"Know this, my beloved brothers: let every person be quick to hear, slow to speak, slow to anger."

But what about in conflict? Still listen instead of speak? Most of the time, yes.

There's one question I can ask that defuses a situation faster than anything (parenting or otherwise):

"Explain to me why you feel/think that way? I want to understand."

It's that simple.

We all want to be understood, not lectured.

Truth be told, listening more than I speak is terribly difficult for me, especially as a mom. I am not trying to imply that I have figured everything out. But I do know that there is a very different tone to the conversation when I prioritize their words over mine.

And even if I don't get to say everything I want to, I know that I'm not the one who can actually accomplish the work of changing their heart or mind anyway. My job is to aim my children toward Christ[3] and then pray that when they are released, they are on a trajectory in the direction of chasing Jesus.

Don't miss this: Jesus loves your children more than you do. Let that sink in.

You may have given birth to them, but He laid down His life for them.

A Listening Disciple

Can we agree that there's not really a more disrespectful behavior than to disregard someone's thoughts, feelings, or opinions

3. Psalm 127:4.

before you've even heard them out? If you want someone to hear you out, don't others deserve the same courtesy?

Even if what they're saying is not right? (Christians, I'm talking to us!)

Why do we think that debating or arguing will get us anywhere when it comes to introducing someone to Christ anyway? I'm not saying that we don't speak truth, but let's not get sharing truth in love confused with agitated debates.

Here's the difference: We don't need to debate truth—His Word never returns void.[4] We can just speak it, and then ask God to let our words take root. Not only is this a much better approach, but it will require fewer words, which means you'll have more time to listen.

Can you even imagine the impact Christians could have on the world if we went into every conversation being quick to listen—or if you're competitive, winning first place for listening?

We are called to share the Gospel, and many times that will look like some sort of conversation. But please keep in mind that the Holy Spirit does not need us to speak for Him. He actually speaks for us. You aren't doing Him a favor by simply being well-spoken or highly educated. God is doing you a favor by giving you opportunities to be the vessel He uses to accomplish His will.

Christians, our words will not save anyone. Do we get that? God's Word spoken through us, however, just might.

Here's what I can guarantee you: His words will never be self-serving for you. They will not glorify you. And they certainly won't come from any place other than love.

Now knowing that, what if we measured our words up against those three things?

4. Isaiah 55:11.

1. Do these words serve God or serve me?
2. Do these words glorify God or glorify me?
3. Do these words come from love or anything less?

Seeing that should help us quickly identify which words that we use are good and which ones aren't necessary.

"But Somer, if I do that I'm going to have less to say."

Exactly. That's the point.

Dietrich Bonhoeffer said it like this:

"Just as love to God begins with listening to His Word, so the beginning of love for the brethren is learning to listen to them. It is God's love for us that He not only gives us His Word but also lends us His ear. So it is His work that we do for our brother when we learn to listen to him. . . . listening can be a greater service than speaking."[2]

We may be missing out on some huge Gospel opportunities simply because we're talking over them.

It is impossible to fully comprehend the words of someone else while your brain is coming up with its own words. Ask any mother who has ever spent her day listening to, "Mom, Mom, Mommy, Mother, Mooooooom!" (Good luck finishing what you're saying to a friend while you're hearing that in the background.)

God has made it clear that we should let our words be few[5] and to let no corrupting talk come out of our mouths.[6] Listening more than we speak requires us to get quiet in order to do that well.

Christians, especially us. Because often, how we listen to others reflects how we listen to God.

5. Ecclesiastes 5:2.
6. Ephesians 4:29.

Carefully Consider How You Listen

Jesus instructed us to "consider carefully how you listen."[7] And have you ever noticed how often, when Jesus spoke in parables, he would end the story with something like, "He who has ears to hear, let him hear?" John also follows Jesus' example, several times recorded in Revelation.[8]

We may be missing out on some huge Gospel opportunities simply because we're talking over them.

Obviously, Jesus and John were not speaking and writing to crowds where some of the people gathered did not have ears attached to their heads. But not everyone had ears to hear with their hearts.

Jesus told a parable one time about a sower planting seeds. Most often it's referred to as the Parable of the Sower, but really this parable should be called the Parable of the Soils. You see, in the story Jesus told, the sower is the same. The seed is the same too. It's the soil that makes the difference. And the soil is an analogy for spiritual ears.[9]

Soil #1: Distracted Ears (Luke 8:4–5, 12)

This seed was at the mercy of where the wind blew it—and it was trampled on and eventually eaten by birds. In the same way, if you allow what you believe to be determined by whomever you're around in that moment or whatever internet rabbit hole you make your way into, that's not a firm foundation to stand on. Don't hear with distracted ears.

7. Luke 8:18 NIV.

8. Matthew 11:15, Matthew 13:9, Matthew 13:43, Mark 4:9, Luke 8:8, Luke 14:35, Revelation 2:7, Revelation 2:11, Revelation 2:17, Revelation 2:29, Revelation 3:6, Revelation 3:13, Revelation 3:22, Revelation 13:9.

9. Luke 8:4–15.

Soil #2: Stubborn Ears (Luke 8:6, 13)

Rock won't allow seed to take root. Hearing and being convinced is not the same as hearing and being changed. You cannot encounter Jesus and remain the same. Don't hear with stubborn ears.

Soil #3: Anxious Ears (Luke 8:7, 14)

The thorny soil has a promising start, but it is eventually overcome by all the worries, riches, and fleeting pleasures of the world, leaving no room for God. Faith will always take you further than FOMO. Don't hear with anxious ears.

Soil #4: Spiritual Ears (Luke 8:8, 15)

Finally, the seed lands on beautiful soil. Soil that is so rich the seed doesn't have to do anything but be there and take it all in. And that's what God's Word does when it lands on spiritual ears: It grows us and helps us reach our full potential so we can walk out our God-given purpose. We must listen, persevere, and patiently wait for the fruit to come. That's how we hear with spiritual ears.

If listening is hard for you, spiritually or in your everyday life with others, ask God to do a work in you. Ask Him to open your ears to what He has to say. That one thing will overflow into the rest of your relationships. When you listen to God, He'll tell you to listen to His children.

The first step is to open your ears for your Father, and the rest will then come.

Trust me, you don't want to miss what He has to say.

A Prayer for Fast Ears + Slow Words

Father, as I enter Your presence,
Quiet my hands, my heart, my mind,
And the loudness of life that is still moving all around me.
Help me focus solely on You and please, God, speak to me.
Your servant is listening.[10]

Forgive me for the times that I have valued the sound of my own voice over listening to others.
I especially repent for the moments I know I have attempted to talk over You.
I surrender my mouth, my tongue, and my words to You, God.

Take away my need to be noticed, Lord.
Help me to not confuse attention with love.

Even right now, create in me a new heart, a clean heart, a pure heart.[11]
And may the only thing that I give breath and sound to overflow from it alone.

When it comes to my mouth . . .

If my words are not beneficial to Your kingdom,
If my words do not promote unity among believers,
Help me not to just swallow them and be silent.
Transform me by the renewing of my mind and purify my thoughts.[12]

10. 1 Samuel 3:10.
11. Psalm 51:10.
12. Romans 12:2.

When it comes to my ears . . .

Make me a better listener.
Let my ability to listen speak just as loudly of my love
For You and Your children as my ability to tell of it.
Help me to see all of the opportunities that You've put
in my path today,
And help me prioritize the opportunities to learn
Before the times to teach.

God, help me to be careful with my tongue and my
thumbs.
Protect me and those around me from the harm that
my words can do.
Please forgive me for harm I've already caused,
And fill me with the humility I need to seek forgiveness
from those I've wronged.

Father, give me wisdom to know
When to speak and when to listen.

Amen.

10

Serve

Lead

Michelle

Culture says: Leading will make you important.

God says: Serving will make you like Me.

In 2015 I was hosting my second leadership retreat for my job at the time, and I invited our friend, Stuart Henslee, to be one of my guest speakers. I didn't give him a specific topic for his session. I just asked him to come and share his top words of wisdom for leaders, because one of the things I admire about him most is that he isn't just a leader himself; Stuart turns others into leaders. (I bet there are hundreds who would say they're serving in their current role because Stuart invested in them—and he's only in his early forties!)

So Stuart came and spoke to our group of about thirty women, and just as I thought, he absolutely crushed it. I'd heard him speak on leadership dozens of times before, and I still found myself not being able to take notes fast enough.

But my biggest lesson from Stuart that day didn't happen during his session. It was when I planned to send him a thank-you text at the end of the day. Ready to share my top takeaways with him, and to let him know the attendees had already begged for him to come back and speak at next year's event, I realized when I opened my phone that he had already texted me:

Thank you for having me speak today—I really enjoyed it. When you get a moment, will you send me the names and addresses of the attendees so I can thank them for coming?

After a few minutes of confusion, I finally wrote back:

Wait, what?! YOU gave of your time and energy. YOU shared your expertise and experience with us. You have already given so much—we should be the ones thanking you!

And his reply:

HA! But I want to take time to encourage them personally. Not just collectively. No rush—just send the names and addresses over when you can.

I'll admit I was confused. Completely dumbfounded. But I was also incredibly inspired and deeply impacted.

If you've attended a Narrow conference or joined our SWHW online membership, you have received a handwritten thank-you note from our team. Now you know why. This is a small way we carry on the lesson Stuart taught me:

Real leadership doesn't happen on stages but serving in the unseen spaces.

There is a clear distinction in how the world does leadership and how leadership should be done in the kingdom.

World's way: Leadership is the ascent to power.
HIS way: Leadership is the descent to the needs of others.

Why Say Servant Leadership?

I've stopped using the term servant leadership, and it all started when these words stopped me in my tracks:

> "Do not be called leaders."—Jesus[1]

I wasn't sure how I'd skipped over this verse in multiple read throughs of Scripture, so I read it again, secretly hoping I'd misread it. But I hadn't. So I went back up a couple of verses, hoping to find something I'd missed that would help me better understand the context.

Instead, I realized that I had breezed past the word Rabbi (which means Teacher) in a similar warning in Matthew 23:8. So if the above quote didn't rattle you as it did me, maybe this one will:

> "Do not be called Rabbi [Teacher]"—Jesus[2]

As a leader and as a teacher of His Word, I had to know more. So, every morning for the next four months, I read and studied Matthew 23:1–12 on repeat, and it radically changed me in so many ways.

1. Matthew 23:10 NASB.
2. Matthew 23:8 NASB.

Before you panic, like I did, Jesus did not say "do not lead" or "do not teach." He said, "do not be called leaders" and "do not be called Rabbi." Teaching and leadership alone do not automatically create trouble.

But often, titles do. Titles have the potential to reinforce our fleshly bend toward pride and self. A case in point being how Jesus continues in His admonishment and charge to the Pharisees (the original audience of this text):

> The greatest among you shall be your servant. Whoever exalts himself will be humbled, and whoever humbles himself will be exalted.
>
> Matthew 23:11–12

Jesus clearly states that the way to be great is by being a servant. So why would we coin the phrase servant leadership other than as an attempt to appease our own egos?

From Founder to First Servant

Servant certainly wouldn't turn many heads if that title were listed in bold on a job board. However, we're not supposed to pursue work that turns heads, but to pursue work that turns hearts.

And before we set the goal to turn someone else's heart, our own heart must turn first.

For years I joked about not liking my job title as founder of She Works HIS Way, mainly because I typically assume most founders are dead. But given our shared leadership model and my own awareness of how quickly my ego can get in the way, I stuck with founder over other titles like CEO or president.

But one day, as I was revisiting Matthew 23, it struck me: Forget founder. I should be first servant!

Not because I'm first in importance. Or first in making decisions. Or because I got here first. But because whenever I look at my job title, I want to be reminded that in order for me to lead this in a way that brings God glory and others good, I must be first to serve.

Talk about a title that's hard to live up to. Makes CEO seem simple. Being first to serve goes against almost every natural inclination we have.

Being a servant requires humility.

Being a servant implies sacrifice.

And that's exactly why being a servant is the only way to lead like Christ.

I can't encourage you enough to dig into Matthew 23:1–12 yourself to let the Holy Spirit do His thing, but these are the top lessons I walked away with from my study:

Let God Select Your Seat

Jesus noted that the scribes and the Pharisees "have seated themselves in the chair of Moses."[3] Whether that was a physical chair doesn't matter. What we know for sure is that Moses' chair would have been the most important earthly seat available in the minds of these religious leaders.

It reminds me of another parable Jesus told, recorded in Luke 14. Jesus is discussing etiquette at a wedding feast. Tradition held that the more important you were, the higher up you would sit at the dinner table. So Jesus instructed that rather than assuming the most important seat is for you, recline at the last place. And should the person who invited you want you to move up the table, they will come and move you higher.

3. Matthew 23:2 NASB.

Don't set your mind on a certain seat. Find a place to serve, and let God promote you if He chooses.

SERVICE > status.

Let God select your seat.

Obey to Follow God, Not to Look Good

That word phylacteries in Matthew 23:5 refers to small cases containing Scripture that were typically worn on the left arm and the forehead. They were supposed to be a personal reminder of God's Word, but the Pharisees had turned them into a public spectacle to draw attention to their spiritual devotion, as is pointed out in the verse: "They do all their deeds to be seen by others."[4]

Again, note that this doesn't say, "Don't do anything that others might notice."

We've talked a lot about humility already, and for good reason. But in Christian circles, humility is often incorrectly applied. Humility doesn't require you to hide, but to act in God's power, not your own.

In fact, one of my favorite examples of humility in Scripture may surprise you:

> And David danced before the Lord with all his might.
>
> 2 Samuel 6:14

For the king, dancing was undignified. And worshiping, indicating there was something greater than you, was something kings typically didn't do.

But David wasn't concerned with being undignified. He wasn't worshiping to be noticed; he was worshiping because God is worthy of being worshiped.

4. Matthew 23:5.

So I define humble action for myself using this verse:

And Michelle ___________ before the Lord with all her might.

These two questions can help reveal if we're motivated by being noticed:

Does your boldness change when people are watching? Humble action is done with all your might, not holding back.

Do you need others watching to do something? Humble action is done before the Lord and no one else.

Let's refuse to do the right thing for the wrong reason. Don't do it to be noticed.

Love God Far More Than You Love Leadership

> They love the place of honor at banquets and the seats of honor in the synagogues, and personal greetings in the marketplaces, and being called Rabbi by the people.
>
> Matthew 23:6–7 NASB

Plainly put, Jesus is calling them out for serving in religious leadership because they loved popularity, importance, approval, and titles. And the more they loved the lesser things, they more they neglected their love for God . . . so much so that the Pharisees couldn't recognize Jesus when He was right in front of their face.

Leadership is a good thing. We need those who are willing to lead. But we need leaders who love God, not merely leaders who love leadership.

Because loving leadership is wrapped up in loving the perks: accepting the award, getting the corner office with a view, having influence over others, calling the shots, being the one with the microphone while others are listening, etc. And while all of those things sound glamorous, they're a far cry from what a day in the life of a leader actually looks like.

While all leaders must be willing to do it, you are not likely to find one who loves accepting the blame for the failure, sacrificing her own comfort for those in her care, or having her strengths expected and her weaknesses scrutinized.

Yet those are very real parts of leadership that no leader gets a pass on. Consequently, the more you love the perks, the more likely you are to hate the actual work.

But again, this is where the world's view of leadership as the ascent to power paints a false picture of what to expect as a leader. Leadership can't be about what you get; that's consumerism. We must stop confusing leadership with consumerism.

Our love for God is what will motivate us to keep leading in the moments when we don't love leadership—and as a leader, you must prepare yourself for there to be far more problems to solve than perks to enjoy.

Be willing to lead, but love God far more than you love leadership.

Be a Sister

My oldest son, Noah, is ten, and he struggles with wanting to be in charge of his little brother and sister. And in his desire to lead and be in control, he often oversteps his role as their big brother, and he tries to "parent" them—right in front of me!

"Noah!" I said one day, unsuccessfully attempting to hide my frustration. "Please just be his brother! He already has two parents, but he only has one brother. So I promise, I will parent him, but I need you to be his brother."

And instantly, a wave of conviction came over me, as the Holy Spirit recalled Matthew 23:8 to my mind:

"But do not be called Rabbi, for One is your Teacher, and **you are all brothers**" (emphasis added).

I began to wonder, How many times, Michelle, could God have said the same words to you that you just said to Noah? How many times have you overstepped your role in the lives of others?

Be willing to lead, but love God far more than you love leadership.

More than I care to count, that's for sure.

Real question: When it comes to those around you, do you view yourself as her spiritual sister or as her spiritual superior?

Siblings love. Superiors are above. And I don't think I need to go into more detail for all of us to realize that there is a large difference between leading in an "I love you" way vs. leading in an "I'm above you" way.

The cross is our equalizer. We're all sinners in need of a Savior. Yes, some have been walking with the Lord longer, but when it comes to how we view ourselves and others, this must remain:

We are spiritual siblings. Jesus is the only spiritual superior.

Be a sister.

Be a Servant

Being a sister is how we ensure we stay under God, as He is the only spiritual superior.

Similarly, being a servant is how we stay under those we lead. (Lest we risk getting above them—and when you get above others, you will default to looking down on them.)

Consider this analogy. Have you ever seen a military team tackle a climbing wall in training? If you haven't, find a video on YouTube to watch. (There are hundreds!) But the quick, impressive, and successful attempts all utilize the same strategy:

More teammates remain on the bottom as long as possible in order for everyone to get over the wall in the quickest, most efficient way. In a team of nine, three teammates go up first, while the remaining six divide into pairs to support the first three over the wall. And from there, everyone but the last two teammates gets the support of two teammates underneath them to ensure the firmest foundation and the strongest start for the climb.

Make the decision to give your strongest support by staying under those you lead rather than attempting to rise above them.

In summary, the strategy is anchored in having support coming from underneath so everyone gets to the top, until the very last teammate when that's no longer an option. The last resort is to rely on the strength coming from the top of the wall.

The same is true for leadership. Make the decision to give your strongest support by staying under those you lead rather than attempting to rise above them.

As John Piper put it, "If God has called you to something high, go low."[1]

Be a servant.

Get Low + Stay Low

It's not just a matter of getting low once, though. It's staying low, when the temptation will regularly present itself for you to elevate yourself, so we must remember Jesus' words:

"Whoever exalts himself shall be humbled; and whoever humbles himself shall be exalted."[5]

So, when God calls you to something high, such as an increase in your influence, here are five principles to get low and stay low:

5. Matthew 23:12.

#1: If your personal competence increases, increase your dependence on God.

Typically, when competence increases, dependence usually decreases. Think about it: You don't return to training wheels after you learn to ride a bike without them. Once you learn how to drive to a certain location, you no longer depend on your Maps app for turn-by-turn directions.

Spiritually, though, it's not the same. God did not create us to be self-sufficient. He created us to need Him. So yes, make the goal to increase in competence. But as competence increases, maintain a high level of dependence on Him.

#2: If your public platform increases, increase your private devotion.

The quickest way to minimize yourself, on or off a platform, is to magnify God. Regularly reminding yourself who God is will simultaneously remind you who you are not.

So read and meditate on God's Word not just to get something for yourself but to cultivate your personal relationship with God.

Pray not because you need something but because you love talking to Him and you're desperate for Him to speak.

Worship not just when you're at church with your hands held high, but behind closed doors offer your life as a full and living sacrifice.

Serve not because it will serve you in some way, but be God's hands and feet by serving someone who can do nothing for you in return, and do it quietly, without receiving any credit.

#3: If the crowd increases, increase community.

People often talk about how lonely leadership is, but lonely leadership is a choice—and not a smart one. If the crowd increases, pull a few people in closer, don't push them away. After all, the deepest ministry you'll ever do is intimate and individual, not public and general.

The test of the strength of your community is not how many people you have around you, but how many people can speak truth into your life and call you out when you're wrong.

Jesus is the only One who never made a mistake. No matter how good a leader you are, from time to time, everyone needs to be corrected. So if no one ever corrects you, and we've already established that you're not perfect, you don't have real community.

You don't have to let everyone in, but you must let someone in. In fact, the first problem God realized existed in the perfect world He created was that it was "not good for the man to be alone."[6] So God created Eve.

Whether you have a crowd around you or not, you were created for community. Don't attempt to live without it.

#4: If your responsibility increases, increase shared leadership.

Kingdom leaders don't collect more followers; they cultivate more leaders.

> Then he said to his disciples, "The harvest is plentiful but the workers are few. Ask the Lord of the harvest, therefore, to send out workers into his harvest field."
>
> Matthew 9:37–38 NIV

As the work increases, build up those around you and share the load. Many operate as though the litmus test of leadership

6. Genesis 2:18 NIV.

is how many people you lead, but true leaders lead through other leaders and refuse to take on the full load alone.

See others the way God sees them: as His treasured creation. Then believe in them in such a way that they begin to get glimpses of how God views them. Put in the time to teach them what you've learned along the way. Do your part to help pull out what God already put in them.

#5: If opportunity increases, increase your focus.

Opportunity always looks good, but it might not align with the mission. Measure every opportunity up against the mission, and you may realize that some opportunities are actually obstacles.

I love the way my friend Angela Mader says it: "Don't let what you're capable of get in the way of what you're called to."[2]

Wouldn't it be sad to let our capability be what stops us from doing what God calls us to do?

Capable does not always equal called. Can does not always equal should. Just because it's logical, that doesn't mean it's the Lord's.

In summary:

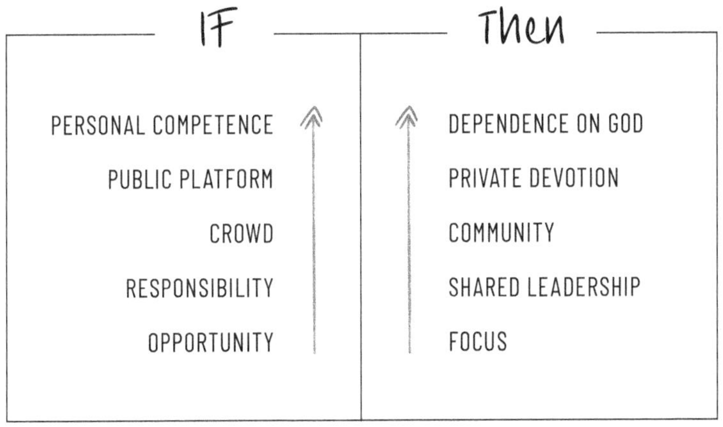

Teach + Lead

Once again, if God has called you to teach, please teach. Some must teach because others need to be taught. If God calls you to lead, please lead! Some must lead because others need to be led.

But at the end of the day, siblings always fall short when they try to be the parent. So instead of trying to overstep our God-given role, we will be much more effective for one another when our goal is to serve God and others as a spiritual sister versus attempting to lead as a spiritual superior.

Quick reminders to put this into practice:

- *Recognize Jesus as the only One with spiritual superiority.*
- *Lay down your need for an earthly title and be secure in your eternal identity.*
- *Remain teachable—by God and by other believers.*
- *Get low and stay low.*
- *When you teach and lead, keep God's glory and serving others—not yourself—as the focus.*

A Prayer to Serve, Not to Be Served

Father, I praise You for being my Leader and my
Teacher.
Forgive me for the times when I've made it more about
my title
Than I make it about Your title.
Make me like Your Son, who came not to be served,
But to serve and to give His life as a ransom for
many.[7]

Shatter my ego, Lord.
Remove my view of leadership that includes power and
perks,
And take away titles and tasks that make it about me.
Help me to see leadership solely as lowering myself to
the needs of others,
And give me boldness to serve in spaces no one sees but
You.

It doesn't matter what seat You select for me, Lord,
I am just so grateful to have a place at Your table.
Expose my motives when I act to be noticed,
And purify me to pursue right actions for the right
reasons.

But God, in the moments that You do call me to lead,
Keep me in step with Your Spirit,
Never running ahead or lagging behind.
Help me to love You far more than I love leading.

And even if the world calls me a leader,
Lord, I just want to be Your follower.

7. Matthew 20:28.

Remind me that following You
Is all I will ever need to lead.

Forgive me for the times when I've attempted to fill
Your role.
Stay above me and give me humility to get low and stay
low.
Do not let me overstep my role as spiritual sister.
You are our only Superior, God.

Send me a strong circle of community, Lord,
Those who will encourage me when leading is hard,
Those who will correct me when I am wrong,
And those who will remind me of Who You are and
what You say.

Raise up other leaders who will lead radically for You,
Mobilize us like an army with a unified mission.
Make us far more familiar with washing feet than
standing on stages,
More content with obscurity than in fame,
More satisfied in You than with recognition.

When others look to me or praise me,
Give me the wisdom to keep my eyes on You.
When others criticize and scrutinize me,
Give me the wisdom to keep my eyes on You.
Every day of life You give me,
My "yes" is Yours to use.

Amen.

11

Give

Earn

Somer

Sacrifice

When you're writing a book, the online thesaurus quickly becomes your best friend. While preparing to write this chapter and thinking through what it means to truly sacrifice (godly generosity usually looks like sacrifice!), I typed in "sacrifice," hoping to get a list of inspiring words that would spark something in my brain.

Instead, as I scrolled down the page, I was caught off guard by the antonyms that were given: increase and rise.

I understood how the opposite of sacrifice could be increase, but what about rise?

Without explanation, I asked my husband to explain why rise is an antonym for sacrifice. Pondering for a moment, he said, "Well, if to sacrifice is to lay something down, it would make sense that the opposite of sacrifice would be to make something rise or to elevate it."

Sacrifice is the opposite of elevation. Sacrifice looks like . . . well it doesn't look like anything—because it's not elevated enough to be seen.

And that's the point.

To give is to be generous, godly generosity is sacrificial, and sacrifices are typically not seen.[1] This may explain why giving is usually hard for us. We enjoy a pat on the back or a social media shoutout when we do something good—especially something sacrificial.

Yes, quietly giving out of our abundance is hard. But have you tried quietly giving to the point of sacrifice? Yikes.

Let me explain it this way. Do you love French fries? (I know, strange segue, but stay with me.)

I like French fries a lot. Cheap fries, fancy fries, I've not met a fried potato I didn't like. So, let me explain sacrificial giving like this . . .

It's one thing for me to share my French fries with my kids when I'm too full to finish them myself, but it's an entirely different story to ask me to share my fries with them when I'm really hungry. It's a struggle, I'm not going to lie.

Truthfully though, how often have you told God, "Give me just a little longer, my generosity is coming and it's going to be great . . ."

Just as soon as we have our emergency fund built up.

Just as soon as we pay off our debt.

Just as soon as I get that raise.

The problem with that mindset, though, is that generosity doesn't just apply to those who have enough to share easily.

1. Matthew 6:1.

Generosity is a commandment for right now, not a choice you can make when it's comfortable or convenient.

Take the story of the widow who gave everything she had in Luke 21:

> Jesus looked up and saw the rich putting their gifts into the offering box, and he saw a poor widow put in two small copper coins. And he said, "Truly, I tell you, this poor widow has put in more than all of them. For they all contributed out of their abundance, but she out of her poverty put in all she had to live on."
>
> Luke 21:1–4

Growing up, I always felt sorry for this widow. Of course I was also inspired by her sacrificial offering, but what I pictured in my mind, I think, may have been wrong this whole time.

Maybe it's because I'm older or maybe it's because I've gotten a front-row seat to God's faithfulness in my own life over the last few years, but I don't feel sorry for her anymore. I don't picture her as the defeated, poor, sad woman I used to envision. Now, it should be noted here that this is my opinion, but I believe that the poor widow gave all that she had because her faith in God was bigger than her fear of poverty. I believe she gave until it hurt because she knew that was the only way to make it stop hurting. And I believe this widow may have had less financial provision than any of the others who gave, but she was by far the wealthiest person in the room!

So doesn't it make sense that a woman like that probably would have skipped to the altar with joyful tears in her eyes and thankfulness in her heart?

Yes, sacrificial giving is giving until it hurts, but I think we need to clarify that we mean an earthly hurt—to be quickly followed up with a heavenly joy! And I don't know about you, but I think that as believers we should be much more interested in forever joy than we are in right-now comfort.

This widow had faith. The kind of faith that makes everything else look so small! Like, micro. Especially earthly wealth and possessions.

She had to have known that the best way to experience God's faithfulness is by putting Him in charge of everything. You see, giving out of our abundance acknowledges ourselves as our provider. But this widow's sacrificial gift acknowledged God as her Provider.

Her Jehovah-jireh.

And do you know where that name originated in Scripture?

Do you remember in Genesis 22, when God asked Abraham to place his son Isaac on the altar? (I brought this story up earlier in chapter 5, Obedience.) It was an intense story. But right before the unimaginable was to take place, God interrupts Abraham and tells him he does not have to sacrifice his son because he has proven he fears God more than anything else.

Here's the cool part that we sometimes leave out, though.

As soon as Abraham looks up after God tells him not to kill Isaac, he sees a ram caught in a thicket and he immediately knew that God not only spared his son's life but provided His own sacrifice, this ram instead of Isaac.

And Scripture says (Genesis 22:14) that Abraham called that place "The Lord will provide."

The first time in Scripture we saw God referred to as Jehovah-jireh.

Listen, if Abraham can trust God with the life of his child, and a poor widow can trust God with her last dime, what's our excuse?

We serve the same God. The God who spared Isaac and provided a ram. The God who saw the widow and took care of her needs. He's our God too. But He cannot be our Jehovah-jireh on a part-time basis or with just a portion of our life.

What Does Jesus Say?

God knew it would be against our nature to give away more than we keep, which is why money is one of the most frequent topics in Scripture. Not because God is greedy, but because money is a top competitor for our heart.

Whenever we find Jesus talking about money in Scripture, and He talked about it a lot (sixteen of Jesus' thirty-eight parables concerned the handling of money and possessions), you won't find Him insulting the wealthy or shaming the poor. But rather, knowing that money is one of the most common sources people turn to for security, He consistently points to the truth that stuff can't satisfy—only He can! And when we have earthly security in money and we have less reason to depend on Him, it's easier for our hearts to be led astray.

It's fine to have money.[2]
It's dangerous to depend on money.[3]
It's a sin to love money.[4]
God loves cheerful givers.[5]

Wise Investing

Thanks to the clear instruction in Scripture, most of us have been taught by our pastors and church leaders that being generous is a mark of a true believer. And although the world doesn't necessarily say generosity is a bad thing, it does present its own

2. Philippians 4:11–13.
3. Matthew 6:24.
4. 1 Timothy 6:10.
5. 2 Corinthians 9:6–7.

caveat that has complicated biblical generosity for many of us. The common message coming from financial experts is that we should save first, invest second, and only then is it "responsible" to start giving our money away.

While the Bible does encourage both saving money[6] and making wise investments,[7] it should be noted that neither is to be put ahead of generosity.[8] Yet when Christians talk finances, we tend to make savings and investments the major issues and barely make generosity a footnote. In addition, many of us have a misunderstanding of what the term *investment* means—but more on that in a minute.

And do you know what else? In the twenty-page list of investment options I've been handed by money gurus, I've never been told that to "Give it away as the Holy Spirit leads" is a viable investment plan.

But wait, Somer, I give to charity, you might be thinking.

Great! But my point is, at the end of the year when you take a look at your financial documents, you'll see your charitable donations listed as just that: charitable donations. But biblically speaking, charitable donations should fall under the investment category.

Generosity is the best and wisest investment plan.

Generosity is the best and wisest investment plan.

Look it up. Multiple times, Scripture tells us that giving away what we have will yield the highest return on our investment (Matthew 19:21; 1 Timothy 6:18–19; Matthew 13:44).

So why isn't this talked about more?

6. Proverbs 13:22, Luke 14:28, Proverbs 21:5.

7. Proverbs 31:16.

8. Acts 20:35; Luke 6:38; Proverbs 11:24–25; Luke 21:1–4; Proverbs 19:17; 1 Timothy 6:17–19; 2 Corinthians 9:6; 1 John 3:17; Psalm 112:5; Deuteronomy 15:7–8; 2 Corinthians 9:11; Acts 2:45; Hebrews 13:16; Proverbs 11:24.

Because our view of money, generosity, and wealth is incredibly skewed by our worldview. In order to be able to see these truths and live them out, we have to see money through the lens of eternity.

An Eternal Perspective

Real question: How do you see the world?

Before we dig into generosity any further, we need to back up and tackle the overarching issue of how we see the world. There is a large difference between worldview (and I'm using this term to cover all the kinds of worldviews that are not Christian) and a Christian worldview. Depending on which lens you look through, you will see generosity and money in almost completely opposite ways.

So, if most of the readers of this book are believers, why do we have to address this? Shouldn't all Christians have a Christian worldview?

In short, yes. We should. But having a Christian worldview doesn't happen automatically at salvation. Developing this mindset takes intentional effort, especially when most of our daily lives are spent out in the "real world."

Even Peter, Jesus' loyal disciple, didn't always get it right.

It is recorded that when Jesus predicts His death and shares this news with the disciples, Peter is not having it.

So much so that Peter takes Jesus aside and begins to rebuke Him. (Yes, Him as in Jesus!)[9]

Bad idea, Peter. Look at how Jesus responds:

"But when Jesus turned and looked at his disciples, he rebuked Peter. 'Get behind me, Satan!' he said. 'You do not have in mind the concerns of God, but merely human concerns.'"[10]

9. Mark 8:31–32.
10. Mark 8:33 NIV.

Jesus didn't exactly hide that He was not okay with what Peter had to say. And why did Jesus react so strongly, to the point of calling Peter "Satan"? Well, for one, not having "in mind the concerns of God but merely human concerns" is a big deal.

Peter did not have an eternal perspective in that moment. He couldn't make sense of why Jesus was going to have to suffer and die.

And in our human nature, we might think that not wanting Jesus to go to the cross is not something that would warrant such a strong rebuke. However, this exchange shows us just how important it is that we recognize the difference between our thoughts and God's thoughts. Between worldview and Christian worldview.

Developing a Christian worldview is like putting in a pair of contacts. It takes a few blinks to get them in place, then it takes a few moments for your eyes to adjust to having them in before you can see clearly. And you have to put them in every day.

We must have the same perspective over our hearts and mind.

The difference between a worldview and a Christian worldview is this:

Worldview sees only right now, centers on me, stores up, and focuses on my earthly impact.

Christian worldview sees eternity, centers on God, gives away, and focuses on my kingdom impact.

Our Choices Are Shaped by Our Worldview

Every decision we make is filtered through one of those two views. So when we struggle to make a decision or find ourselves in that terribly uncomfortable tension of not being sure which way to go, it's more than likely because your worldview and your Christian worldview are both fighting for dominance.

Look back at the choices you made last week. You may or may not feel that you made any life-altering decisions, but the daily decisions we make often add up to a greater impact than we realize.

What/who got your best?

What/who got your leftovers?

What did you spend money on?

What did you make room for on the calendar and what got the boot?

Our choices do a much better job at revealing our priorities than our spoken words or our unspoken intentions. So don't just gloss over those questions. Answer them honestly.

Then ask yourself this: Do your answers reflect those of a woman whose priority is kingdom impact?

A note to my overthinkers . . .

If you who absolutely despise making any and all life decisions due to your inability to just make a choice (I'm the mother of a chronic overthinker, so I get you!), maybe I can offer you this to help:

Could it be that your struggle with overthinking is really just a lens issue?

Maybe the reason you feel like you can't make a decision is because you're trying to see the situation simultaneously through both lenses—both your worldview and your Christian worldview.

Can you imagine lifting a set of binoculars to your eyes only to see that one of the lenses had you seeing everything upside down? Wouldn't that make it terribly difficult to figure out what you were looking at so you could navigate your way forward? No doubt you'd take a lot more time to consider before you'd be willing to take a step.

But if you'd just close the eye that's looking through the upside-down lens, everything would be crystal clear.

Maybe it's time to destroy the lens that is forcing you to evaluate the what-ifs and worst-case scenarios outside of God's plan. I'd be anxious about those too! One of the greatest perks of being a Christ-follower is allowing Him to guide you through your choices.

So how do you close your eyes to a worldview that is confusing your everyday life and sabotaging your choices? How do you actually begin to see what's right in front of you from an eternal perspective?

By treasuring God above all else.

Because yes, your choices are shaped by your worldview, but your worldview is shaped by what we treasure. And "where your treasure is, there your heart will be also."[11]

But I Earned It

Couldn't one argue that the more money we earn, the more money we are able to give, making earning money a really good thing?

Yes.

But the problem with earning more is not in the accruing of money, but the ownership of our money.

You see, we are not to look at our money as our money. That's why Scripture doesn't call money itself evil, but says that loving money is evil.[12]

You've probably heard the biblical account of the Rich Young Ruler[13] in teachings about money. It is a very poignant but clear-cut story: A young man asks Jesus what he must do to have

11. Matthew 6:21.
12. 1 Timothy 6:10.
13. Matthew 19:16–30.

eternal life. Jesus first answers to keep His commandments. With pride, the young man says he has kept all of the commandments since he was a boy. This is where the story changes.

Jesus challenges him to sell all of his possessions, give to the poor, and come follow Him. And the young man walks away, sad.[14] He really believed that his stuff was his stuff. That was the entire issue.

As we read this account, it's easy for us to think, Come on, man, you're talking to Jesus! You obviously should choose Him over your possessions.

But do we?

Also, the story doesn't end there, even though that's usually where it stops when we tell it. As soon as the young man leaves, Peter speaks up and says (my paraphrase), "Hey Jesus, we've left everything and followed you, so what do we get?"[15]

Jesus replies with, "A hundredfold" and "eternal life."[16] Pretty sweet deal!

And this is another one of those instances where, if we read our Bible in chapters and verses instead of as a continuous story, we might miss that the parable Jesus teaches next isn't a different day or a different scene but continues the conversation moments after the young man left.

The parable of the laborers in the vineyard[17] is not out of the blue but is an extension of Jesus' response to Peter's question. Jesus is making a point that the kingdom of heaven is very different from other kingdoms—almost completely opposite, actually.

In summary, early one morning, the master of a house goes out to find laborers to work in his vineyard. He found a few

14. Matthew 19:21–22.
15. Matthew 19:27.
16. Matthew 19:29.
17. Matthew 20:1–16.

men, negotiated the wages for the day, and they went to work. The master ends up going out to look for more laborers at the third hour, the sixth hour, the ninth hour, and get this—the eleventh hour. He hires more guys with only one hour left in the workday. At the end of the day, he gathered all the laborers so that he could give them their pay. Much to the all-day workers' surprise, each man earns the same wages. Even the ones who only worked an hour.

Needless to say, that did not go over well. So how did the master respond? Reminding them that he was doing no wrong—he paid the all-day workers what they agreed to, and he chose to be generous with the last-added workers. Then he drilled in the idea that generosity is making the last first and the first last.[18]

God doesn't see money the way we see it. He himself is the standard for just and fair, so we cannot argue that this parable is unfair.

Remember the two lenses? This is another reason we have to be incredibly serious about looking through the right one. Peter's question wasn't bad (although it was a bit self-serving), but Jesus answered him with two parts that each of us needs to grasp for ourselves:

#1: If you give up everything to follow Jesus, you will get a hundredfold and eternal life.

#2: Don't get too cozy, though. This is not about your doing something good and getting something good. It's about His grace and what should be your most reasonable response to what Jesus has done for you.

Jesus wanted to make it clear that leaving everything behind and following Him didn't earn them anything in return, but because He is so good, we still get something. Something really amazing.

18. Matthew 20:13–16.

In order to be good stewards of your money, and to give until it hurts, you're going to have to flip the cultural construct of work, wealth, and financial planning completely on its head.

It won't be easy, but when you begin to see your money as a resource God gives you to further His mission rather than your earnings to secure your future, you will:

- *Give more*
- *Love bigger*
- *Be more grateful*

And, no doubt, you will see God's hand at work in even more ways in your life.

Given, Not Earned

The story of Mary, the mother of Jesus, is usually just told at Christmas, but a few years ago, I realized there is so much to be learned from her example. Especially to learn about what it looks like to be chosen and favored by God.

Let me tell you: It doesn't look the way you think it would.

Mary was poor. Like, really poor. Scholars tell us she was more than likely uneducated and barefoot. Shoes would have been a luxury to her. She was probably between the ages of thirteen and fifteen, and she was engaged to a young man named Joseph. They were from the town of Nazareth—a poverty-stricken slum.[19]

When the angel, Gabriel, came to Mary to tell her she was going to give birth to Jesus, his opening statement was, "Greetings, O favored one."[20]

19. John 1:46.
20. Luke 1:28.

So often, though, when we think of being favored, we think of having material things. But even after giving birth to Jesus, Mary was still poor by the world's standards.

Here's how we know this: When it was time to take Jesus to Jerusalem so they could present Him to the Lord at the Temple, it says they could take either a pair of turtledoves or two young pigeons.[21] The law of Moses that established this custom back in the Old Testament stated that the sacrifice to be offered when presenting your firstborn to the Lord was actually supposed to be a lamb.[22]

So why did Mary and Joseph have two different options? Because the law also offered a stipulation for those who were too poor to afford a lamb.[23]

Mary, the chosen one, the favored one, the mother of Jesus, qualified for the poor people's sacrifice.

Ironic, isn't it? Our human nature wants to think giving birth to the Messiah would come with some financial perks. But no.

You see, God's definition of favor is so wildly different from ours. Because being given favor actually means to be given grace. Favor is grace.

Mary may have been poor, but she was favored. And this was before she had done anything to even "deserve" that favor. Mary had favor with God before she was given an assignment and before she responded.

Let that sink in: We serve God from a place of *being* favored, not from a place of *earning* favor.

And God's favor in our lives is visible in a way that glorifies God, not us.

In modern-day America, we would look at a young couple like Joseph and Mary and feel badly for them. Not only that,

21. Luke 2:22–24.
22. Exodus 13:13.
23. Leviticus 5:7.

we'd expect that they felt bad for themselves too. But there is no record of Mary and Joseph ever complaining. They were content because God was meeting all of their needs and they were raising His Son.

So, let's be very careful not to assume wealth equals importance. If status is what you're after, you might fool a couple of, well, fools, with your bank account balance, but God is not impressed.

God's favor in our lives is visible in a way that glorifies God, not us.

Wealth doesn't qualify you for anything more than greater generosity. To whom much is given, much is required.[24]

Is it okay to have wealth? Absolutely! It is no more a sin to be wealthy than it is a sin to be poor. But wealth comes with a weighty responsibility to serve others in a way that many can't. If God has blessed you financially, I hope that motivates you and makes you really excited.

See a Need, Meet a Need

If you knew me personally, you would know just how ironic it is that I am writing anything about planning because I am about as far away from a planner as one can be. To be fair, though, planning and productivity are different; so, planners, stay with me because you're going to love what God has taught me recently on the subject of generosity.

The best way to find yourself available to be spontaneously used by God in the area of generosity is to plan to be generous. Godly stewardship includes generosity, and spontaneous generosity requires good stewardship.

At my church (South Shore Church—if you're in or around Annapolis, MD, come see us!), we have a phrase we say a lot:

24. Luke 12:48.

See a need, meet a need.

I think it is probably pretty self-explanatory, but this is why it's so important: God has given each of us our own circles of influence. These circles include our family, friends, co-workers, Amazon delivery guy, hair stylist, barista, etc.

The people who are in your life or who keep showing up over and over again are not randomly placed there. They are your neighbors,[25] as Scripture refers to them. These are the people you are to love more than you love yourself, which means if you see that they are in need, it is your responsibility to help them. If believers all took care of our own circles this way, the number of people in need would decrease drastically, increasing the opportunity for God to be glorified drastically. Because when Christians meet the needs of others, they always meet them with Jesus.

Bottom line: The world will not necessarily be changed by there simply being more rich women. But if this world had more generous women? Now, that could make an impact.

In a world of extravagant lifestyles, let's aim for extravagant generosity instead.

See a need? Meet a need.

25. Mark 12:31.

A Prayer to Serve God, Not Money

Father, all that I have is Yours.
Nothing belongs to me.
Recall that to my mind often so I remain both aware of
and grateful
for each and every blessing You lavish on me.
Every good thing comes from You.[26]

Help me live with open hands that freely share what
You've given to me,
Remembering that only open hands, not closed fists,
receive from You.
Forgive me for the times when I act selfishly or stingily,
and the moments when I am entitled and dissatisfied.
Open my ears to the Holy Spirit's prompting.
Give me an opportunity to be generous today.

Take the blessing and provision that You have given me
And use it to further Your mission, not my own gain.
Make me ambitious to multiply disciples, not merely
wealth.
Let my life show that I serve You, not money.[27]

When I have much . . .

Make me generous.
Remind me that to whom much is given, much shall be
required,[28]
And that genuine generosity is still sacrificial, not
affordable.

26. James 1:17.
27. Matthew 6:24.
28. Luke 12:48.

Do not allow earning to become my idol,
But make giving my ministry.
Put Your glory on full display in my life.

When I have just enough . . .

Make me more generous.
Remind me that what you've promised is my daily bread, not tomorrow's meals.
Make it my habit to turn tomorrow's worries into today's prayers.
Put Your glory on full display in my life.

When I have less . . .

Make me the most generous.
Use me to do a modern-day loaves and fishes[29] or widow's mite[30] miracle.
Remind me You are all I need.
Put Your glory on full display in my life.

You are Jehovah-jireh, my Provider.
Not my career.
Not my boss.
Not my bank account.
YOU.
I praise You for providing all my needs![31]

Amen.

29. John 6:5–14.
30. Luke 21:1–4.
31. Philippians 4:19.

12

Approved

Approval

Michelle

Culture says: You need to earn others' approval.

God says: Jesus earned the only approval you need.

Growing up, we called it peer pressure. As adults, we make it people-pleasing. The Bible refers to it as "the fear of man."[1] They're all the same, and if it's not dealt with, it's a serious problem—not merely a personality tendency or a minor flaw.

There's nothing wrong with being liked. But we should be cautious when we like being liked—because without the proper guardrails, liking being liked can escalate to needing to be liked—which is dangerous ground. One of Satan's favorite sabotage strategies seems to be how much he can limit kingdom impact by tempting us to hunger for, hear, and hang

1. Proverbs 29:25.

on to other people's opinions of us more than we hunger for, hear, and hang on to God.

Two of the clearest ways to gauge the grip people-pleasing has on you is how you respond to two things: criticism and flattery.

When Crickets Become Critics

If you've ever started something, you know crickets. You pray, you prepare, and you plan, and you finally pour out your passion—only to be met with silence in return. You're dumbfounded. Discouraged. Thoughts begin to race in your mind: Did I hear God right? Does no one else care about this like I do?

I can empathize. Someone not caring about what God gives you doesn't stop at feeling like they don't care for your words; it feels like they don't care about you.

But silence is where most endeavors begin—even godly ones. And slowly, some start to pay attention. And just as you feel like you're building some momentum, you get sucker-punched by what happens next:

Criticism.

All of my entrepreneurial endeavors have somehow involved my faith. What was once faith and fitness eventually developed into faith and work. And people never failed to share exactly what they thought as I gained any form of traction. In fact, for the first year or longer for each endeavor, almost every post generated contradictory messages:

- *Your workouts are great, but I wish you'd tone down the Jesus stuff. Bye.*
- *What does being a Christian have to do with being healthy? I love what you have to say about God, but the fitness stuff feels really out of place. Unfollow.*
- *Yes to the devos, but I don't work . . . so I'm out.*

- *Congrats—you just lost a follower. I thought this page was about my job, not a Bible study.*

One particular time, when the criticism escalated to personal betrayal, quitting crossed my mind. And not in an emotional way, but in a very raw, real way. But in His goodness, while I was contemplating quitting, God reminded me of Jeremiah. Now, there are plenty of stories recounted in the Bible of people who had difficult assignments. And of those, Jeremiah makes my top five.

Process this: He prophesied to Israel for forty years and never saw one person repent and turn to God. Forty years without a yes. Forty years! (For those of you in sales, can you even imagine?!)

Jeremiah recalls that following God's call on his life has resulted in the hatred and mockery of others[2] and his trusted friends watching for his failure and plotting revenge.[3] And although many quit for lesser reasons, Jeremiah didn't give up, even though he honestly wanted to. This is how he put it:

> If I say, "I will not mention him, or speak any more in his name," there is in my heart as it were a burning fire shut up in my bones, and I am weary with holding it in, and I cannot.
>
> Jeremiah 20:9

Basically, Jeremiah tried to quit. But anytime he gave up on what God had called him to, holding in the truth of what God had revealed to him only created greater pain. I mean, fire in his bones is pretty powerful imagery, don't you think?

But Jeremiah's level of commitment might be the best way to decipher what actually is God's calling for your life. Because

2. Jeremiah 20:8.
3. Jeremiah 20:10.

calling has almost become a Christian buzzword, misinterpreted solely as something we do that mutually benefits both God and us.

So here's the question we should ask ourselves: Would you keep doing what you claim God has asked you to do, even if there was nothing in it for you?

Strip away results of any kind. Accolades. Titles. Perks. Platform. Respect. Are you still in?

To be clear, I don't wish Jeremiah's assignment (even a lesser version of it!) on any of us. But I think it's a good exercise to examine our motives and make sure we're not being flippant with that word *calling*.

Because here's the truth: If results can make you quit, you're not working from a place of conviction and calling. This is not to say your life must equal misery. But are you genuinely willing to stick to what God has asked you to do, regardless of what's in it for you?

That's the kind of worker God's mission requires: servants who are so called that quitting creates more pain than failure. It's the kind of worker I needed to be.

So I prayed and committed to quit putting quitting on the table. Because God called me to this, so I will. Period. Then, I prayed for the friend who hurt me. I prayed for God to heal my heart and to keep it soft so I could love the next person well instead of keeping them at an arm's length to avoid getting hurt again. And I asked God for strength to serve stronger.

And guess what God did in the next twenty-four hours? My greatest career betrayal was followed by my greatest career blessing. After two years of begging her to partner with me at She Works HIS Way, Somer called me and said, "I don't know what you need me to do here. And honestly, I don't even know if I can do it. But I won't do that to you. When can I start?"

Talk about an answer to prayer. To this day, every day that Somer and I (and the rest of the SWHW team!) work together,

I serve stronger in this mission because we're in it together—because God called each of us here.

Every day that I get to serve this community is a reminder to me of the blessings I would have missed if I'd let criticism cause me to quit.

So don't resent the crickets; let them prepare you for critics. If silence discourages you, critics will destroy you. Ask God to use the silence to strengthen you, to quicken your obedience to His call without distraction, and to focus you on Him alone. Plus, you never know what other plans He has to make "all things work together for good."[4]

And when that happens, the crickets (and yes, even the critics) definitely weren't for nothing.

So here's our reminder as clearly as I can put it:

IT'S OKAY TO QUIT WHAT
GOD CALLS ME TO DO WHEN:

~~I don't feel like doing it anymore.~~

~~Not enough people are paying attention.~~

~~Too many people are criticizing me.~~

~~The betrayal hurts too much.~~

~~It starts costing me personally.~~

God says it's time to move on.

4. Romans 8:28.

Flattery Can Destroy Too

How you respond to negative feedback is actually a good indication of how you will respond to positive feedback. Losing motivation or gaining motivation based on how people respond reveals you are more likely to be swayed by the voice of man than the call of God.

Flattery can be just as deadly to a God-given purpose as criticism.

Perhaps the clearest example of seeing this played out is in the life of King Saul. He went from literally hiding when he was to be announced before Israel as king[5] to a complete glory hog. The people of Israel may as well have had Saul on a puppet string—he did whatever he could to please them.

Check out this reality show-worthy exchange between Saul and Samuel:

> And Samuel said to Saul, "I will not return with you. For you have rejected the word of the Lord, and the Lord has rejected you from being king over Israel."
>
> 1 Samuel 15:26

And that's not even the dramatic part. When Samuel turns to leave, Saul (keep in mind, he's the king!) grabs Samuel by the robe so hard that the robe actually tears.[6] And then the truth comes out:

> Then he said, "I have sinned; yet honor me now before the elders of my people and before Israel, and return with me, that I may bow before the Lord your God."
>
> 1 Samuel 15:30

5. 1 Samuel 10:20–22.
6. 1 Samuel 15:27.

Unlike the first time he asked Samuel to come with him so he could worship God, this time, Saul reveals his real motives. He didn't really want to worship. He was just afraid of what the people would think if Samuel didn't come back with him.

Don't gloss over this too quickly. Saul was so consumed with people's approval that he reduced worshiping the real and holy God to an act of manipulation for his own gain.

The same can happen to us. Any time we fake following God or minimize who God is in exchange for flattery it's not just people-pleasing—it's idolatry. Don't let flattery fool you or rule you to the point that it controls you. What flattery can control, flattery can also ruin.

The life Saul was actually living was drastically different from the image he attempted to portray. No matter how well he could fake being a confident, successful king, he was a man so broken that the only way he could get any rest was if a little shepherd boy would come and play the harp for him.[7] And not just any unknown harp-playing shepherd boy, but David, a man after God's own heart,[8] who would eventually replace Saul as king.

David's reign didn't happen right away, though. Samuel anointed David to be the next king when David was somewhere between ten and fifteen years old. But not even killing Goliath[9] hastened his timeline to the throne. David also endured nine of Saul's attempts on his life—and even refused to take revenge on Saul, whom he deemed the Lord's anointed, when he had the chance.[10]

David could easily have fallen into the flattery trap himself. But despite being anointed as the next king and being given a

7. 1 Samuel 16:14–23.
8. 1 Samuel 13:14.
9. 1 Samuel 17.
10. 1 Samuel 24.

position at the palace at a young age, David continued to go back and forth between the palace and his house so he could tend the sheep,[11] serving the Lord wherever he went. And just as God promised, David became king when he was thirty years old[12]—fifteen to twenty years after being told he would be king.

Remember God's promise that nothing done for Him is wasted.[13] How people respond—whether with silence, criticism, or flattery—doesn't get the final say. God does.

This Is Your Brain on Social Media

In our oversharing online world, it's becoming more and more difficult to free yourself from what others think about you. The approval struggle isn't new, but it's also never been easier to access, evaluate, and even dwell on your approval rating.

Popularity used to be relative, not quantitative. Other than a few times during adolescence did contests or awards like homecoming queen or senior superlatives actually declare a popularity "winner." It's not like that for teens today, though, and we've extended the importance of popularity well into adulthood.

Social media makes it possible to access a nearly instant approval rating. For the last decade, research studies have confirmed that the "reward" center of our brains is more active when others agree with us—including something as simple as a like, double tap, or comment. Increased social media usage has been linked to dissatisfaction and even depression. Scientists have even confirmed that getting a social media notification releases dopamine to your brain—the same pleasure hormone associated with food, exercise, sex, and drugs.

11. 1 Samuel 17:15.
12. 2 Samuel 5:4.
13. 1 Corinthians 15:58.

If you missed the nineties, first of all—I'm sorry. You missed so much, I wish we could go to coffee so I could catch you up. But I vividly remember the nineties "This Is Your Brain on Drugs" commercial campaign that compared the effects of your brain on drugs to a smashed egg in a frying pan. And social media has the same potential.

Before you think I'm exaggerating, there is proof. Brain scans of social media addicts are actually very similar to those of drug-dependent brains.[1]

I'm not going to ask you to delete your accounts. (God might, but I won't!) But I am going to encourage you to exercise caution. Even if God has called you to online responsibilities, you still have to protect yourself against approval addiction. It's not just your brain you're up against, but a real enemy.

These are the social media principles I use to fight against approval addiction:

- » Be more concerned with following God than wondering who is following you.
- » Share content that glorifies God and elevates others.
- » Use social media to connect with others—not to gain popularity.
- » Share what God lays on your heart, not what you think others expect.
- » Don't allow criticism or flattery to change the message God gives you to share.
- » It's not bad to have lots of likes but it is dangerous to like lots of likes and detrimental to need lots of likes.
- » See faces and souls, not followers or numbers.
- » Use each platform like you know your time on earth is short.
- » Consume intentionally, not mindlessly.
- » Take breaks. (If you can't take breaks, that's called an addiction.)

The Heart Test

It is possible to do all the right things for all the wrong reasons. You have the potential to follow the rules without following Christ. That's why we cannot stop at considering our behaviors, but we must examine our motives.

Ever had thoughts like . . .

- *Why isn't anyone impressed by what I'm doing?*
- *No one notices. Maybe I should try something else.*
- *It's hard to keep doing this work without any recognition.*

These are real feelings. But as real as feelings may be, feelings rarely make a good compass. Truth must lead our hearts so thoughts like this don't escalate into pity-party permission but serve as warning signs that we're looking for approval in the wrong place.

When those thoughts begin popping up, I head to Matthew 6:1–7 for these reminders:

Practice righteousness before God, not before people (v. 1). Some of the good you do will be known by others. We can't always do good in secret. In fact, publicly living out your obedience can serve as a powerful witness for others. Public recognition isn't wrong . . . unless it's your motive. If getting noticed by others is the only reason you would do good, that's not obeying God. That's performing for people.

Generosity isn't really generosity if I expect something in return (vv. 2–4).

Even if that something is as simple as applause or even acknowledgment. Generosity, with godly motivations, is an act of worship. Treat it as such.

Even if others can hear, you're talking to God, so mean what you pray (vv. 5–7).

When my middle son was in kindergarten, he was asked to pray in his school's weekly chapel. That night at the dinner table, his older brother asked, "Weren't you nervous? Even the fifth-graders were there!"

Cole replied, "Nope. I wasn't talking to them."

Prayer isn't rhetoric or words that vanish, but a real conversation with God. He hears you,[14] and He still speaks.[15]

Aim to have secrets with God (vv. 4, 6).

Closeness with God is determined by what God, and only God, knows about you.

That's not a threat, by the way, but a perk. Your life is not wrapped up in some religious performance, but in a real God who outlandishly loves you.

The Gospel makes having an intimate, personal relationship with Jesus possible. But intimacy is not a natural byproduct. Intimacy must be pursued. And intimacy grows in small spaces.

I love that this passage calls them secrets. Not "secrets" like whispering behind someone's back or isolating others from the conversation so they feel excluded, but more like surprises that will one day be revealed and celebrated.

It's like that moment when a positive sign pops up on a pregnancy test. I could never keep it a secret for very long, but I have vivid memories of prayers and praise, right there in the bathroom, when this sweet new life growing inside of me was a beautiful secret between me and God.

My three children also represent the kind of gifts God is able to give. I may not know exactly what rewards in heaven look

14. 1 John 5:14–15.
15. John 10:4 NASB; John 14:6.

like, but I am confident I don't want to settle for the world's counterfeit offer.

Approval Is a Faith Issue

We know seeking the approval of others is exhausting, but we often miss how needing approval from people also affects our faith.

Jesus said, "How can you believe, when you receive glory from one another, and you do not seek the glory that is from the one and only God?"[16]

Whom we seek approval from reveals what we believe about God. We can care so much about what other people think about us that we can actually miss who God actually is.

If you've been in Christian circles for a while, you've probably heard this verse:

> For am I now seeking the approval of man, or of God? Or am I trying to please man? If I were still trying to please man, I would not be a servant of Christ.
>
> Galatians 1:10

We've already noted that extremes are often easier, and pleasing people is no exception. Even this well-intended instruction from Paul has created two ditches we can quickly fall into.

Ditch #1: The Christian Jerk

Because some cling extra hard to not being here to please people, Christian jerks twist this verse to grant themselves permission to not care for people. They talk about Jesus, but

16. John 5:44 NASB, emphasis added.

usually it comes across as arrogant or angry. They are quick to replace compassion and grace with sarcasm and snark.

But Paul also wrote this:

> Give no offense to Jews or to Greeks or to the church of God, just as I try to please everyone in everything I do, not seeking my own advantage, but that of many, that they may be saved.
>
> 1 Corinthians 10:32–33

Paul does not contradict himself. Both letters emphasize his commitment to the Gospel. To Galatia, he emphasizes finding approval in God, not people, and to Corinth, he emphasizes pleasing people for the hope of their salvation, not to gain their approval.

Ditch #2: The Anxious Earner

Rather than seeing the cross as Jesus having paid the debt they owed, the anxious earner views his or her Christian "successes" as payment installments and their failures as adding to their debt, as if Jesus keeps a tab open. They don't obey God out of love, but out of guilt. It's not just the approval of others that they attempt to earn, but they try to earn the approval of God too.

I've got some bad news, but I've also got the best news.

The bad news: On your own, you cannot earn God's approval. Your good deeds are like filthy rags.[17] Apart from Christ, we are lost, desperate, and without hope. Keeping all of the law without the blood of Jesus is not enough to get you into heaven.

But here's the best news: On the cross, Jesus earned your approval for you. In His defeat of death, Jesus became not just

17. Isaiah 64:6.

a way, but the Way to reconcile us with God after the separation sin caused.

I know that's not the popular thing to tell you. It would be much more comfortable if I could tell you to pick your path to God. But the one true God is too real to equate with any other path that leads to nowhere.

Living Approved vs. Living for Approval

There is a drastic difference between the readiness of living for God as one who is approved by Him and the insecurity of attempting to live for God and earn approval. The only approval you and I can earn is from one another, and it will never last and never satisfy.

Go back to Jesus' last week on Earth. Mark 11 paints an incredible picture as Jesus entered into Jerusalem. The people shouted, "Hosanna!" They laid their cloaks down and put palm branches down in His path, which was basically a form of our modern-day red carpet. They recognized Him as God's Son, as the Promised One from the line of David. If this happened today, everyone would be begging for selfies, aiming to get a glimpse of Jesus so they could show their friends, "I was there! I saw Him!"

That was Sunday. By Tuesday, the plot to kill Jesus began.[18] And on Thursday evening, Jesus was publicly betrayed by one of his twelve most trusted followers.

Four. Days. Later. Talk about a reality check on pursuing the world's approval. The world's approval is temporary, fleeting, and totally unreliable.

Jesus was arrested and put on multiple trials, shuffled between the high priest, the Sanhedrin, Herod, and Pilate. He was

18. Mark 14:1–2.

scourged and beaten. Peter, one of the three in his inner circle, denied Him three times. The crowd begged to have released to them one of the day's most dangerous criminals instead of Jesus, calling for Jesus' crucifixion.

He was mocked with a crown of thorns, forced to carry His own cross, and had nails driven in his hands and feet to the crowd's pleasure. With the exception of John, Jesus' mother Mary, and a few other women, Jesus was abandoned by those who knew Him, including the remaining disciples, who were afraid they would also be put to death if they hung around.

And there, between two thieves, our sinless Savior died a criminal's death on the cross. Palm Sunday was glamorous, but by Thursday, things had turned bloody. By Friday, Jesus was dead.

But the story doesn't finish on Friday. The crowd's approval did not have the final say, but the Word of God did. Three days later, the tomb was empty, and still today, He is risen!

Approval is not measured in likes, followers, or dollars. Approval is not a bigger platform or a better promotion. And most of all, approval is not something you have to spend your life seeking.

Almost every other world religion is rooted in what you have to do, but following Christ is rooted in what Jesus has done. Approval is what Jesus did for you on the cross. The Gospel is your approval. Jesus earned your approval! Jesus is alive, your approval is sealed, and one day, He is coming back for the approved.

I have to believe that there will be at least one of you who reads these words who has never given your life to Christ. Your first step is simply to say yes to Jesus.

I wish I could be right there by your side, but I know He's with you now. Following Him will not guarantee you the "health, wealth, and happiness" that the world pursues, but living for Him results in peace,[19] freedom,[20] and fullness of joy.[21] Trials are certain,[22] but you will never go through them alone.[23]

I'd so much rather you live a challenging life than an empty one. The decision to live for Christ is the most important decision and the best decision you'll ever make. I am praying right now that before you choose any of the strategies or principles you've read in these pages that you will simply choose Him.[2]

Live As a Believer

I want to leave you with the same charge Paul gave to all the churches:

> Only let each person lead the life that the Lord has assigned to him, and to which God has called him. This is my rule in all the churches.
>
> 1 Corinthians 7:17

That one sentence speaks truth into comparison, complacency, and contentment. Wherever God has you is where God has called you to live as a believer. That's the inscription that gives you both purpose and authority, no matter where you go.

The whole picture of the Bible is actually a great mirror to living the Christian life. There is not a burning bush[24] on every page, but there is always God to glorify and someone to serve.

There's not a single kingdom effort that can happen without some simple task that the world would call meaningless. But nothing is small in the hands of a big God.

19. John 14:27.
20. 2 Corinthians 3:17.
21. Psalm 16:11.
22. James 1:2–4.
23. Deuteronomy 31:6.
24. Exodus 3.

He lets your story weave into His greater story.

His way trumps your way.

Know God more than you aim to be known.

You will gain far more from losing yourself than finding yourself.

Success is obedience.

Let love trump skill.

Put you before me.

Invest in relationships more than achievements.

Aim to serve, not to lead.

Be more intentional with how you listen than how you'll be heard.

Earning is fine but giving is better.

Live as one approved by God to be entrusted with the Gospel.[25]

Leave more evidence that she works HIS way than she works her way.

And let's watch what God can do.

25. 1 Thessalonians 2:4.

A Prayer to Live Approved

Father, forgive me for the times I seek others' approval
Instead of finding approval in You.
Do not let me love the glory that comes from others,
But to only love the glory that comes from You.[26]

God, make me aware when I have grown addicted to approval,
And convict me in how I need to change.
The life you've blessed me with and the charge you've given me
Cannot be reduced to performing for people.

God, free me from dwelling on what others think about me.
Teach me the difference between pleasing people and loving people.
Turn my efforts toward living in gratitude for who You are,
And what You've done in my life.

God, Your foolishness is wiser than men,
And Your weakness is stronger than men.[27]
God, I praise You that people do not get the final say,
But You—my Creator, my Sustainer, and my Redeemer—You do.

Self cannot satisfy.
Human opinion cannot satisfy.
You alone can satisfy me, God.
So, when I feel unsatisfied,
Make it my habit to turn to You.

26. John 12:43.
27. 1 Corinthians 1:25.

Protect me from following my feelings
Or the fickle opinions of others.
But remind me that my approval is sealed in Jesus,
Who died the death I deserved,
And that it's through Him I now live.[28]

God, when I find myself craving approval,
Take me back to the cross.
Remind me that what Jesus did for me
Is the only approval I'll ever need,
And that I did nothing to earn it.

Keep me in awe of the Gospel, Lord.
Help me live as one approved,
A worker who knows Jesus covered all my shame,
And accurately handles Your truth.[29]

Equip me to grow in grace,
And to daily embrace my identity in You.
Give me endurance to run the race You've set before me
With confidence You've already claimed the victory.

Give me a posture of worship
That aims to glorify You in all I do.
Wherever I am,
Help me live as a believer.

Amen.

28. Galatians 2:20.
29. 2 Timothy 2:15.

Epilogue

Michelle + Somer

Culture says: Do it all.

God says: Do what matters.

We have a final confession: One of the most challenging aspects of writing this book for us is that we don't get the opportunity to get to know you personally. If you're a woman who chose to read this, we have no doubt that not only would we be fast friends, but that there's so much we could learn from you.

So we were thinking about how to conclude the book because we pray you'll jump into our community so we can keep the conversation going—just head to sheworksHisway.com and click "Join Now." (We are committed to being your best, but definitely not your biggest, business expense each month!) And we decided that we'd pretend we got to take you out for coffee; after we learned how you came to know the Lord and what He's done in your life, we'd know enough to offer you some personalized encouragement that considers both your identity and your personality.

While the world often makes them one and the same, as a Christ-follower, there is a drastic difference between your identity and your personality.

As far as your identity goes, in Christ, you are a new creation.[1] God has written eternity on your heart,[2] and because of Christ, even now, you are a citizen of heaven.[3] There is nothing you did to earn your new identity that is marked by Christ's righteousness.[4] Your identity is a result of your salvation, which is a gift from God. You are not something because of what you can do on your own, but you now have the potential to be something because of what Christ has done. He is your firm foundation.

Now for your personality. Your new identity in Christ doesn't end your struggle with sin, and it also doesn't erase how God made you. One day, we will be perfected with Him in Heaven. But He still gave you a life to live here on earth. You're still you, but now you have a purpose that extends far beyond you.

Scripture uses imagery of God "forming" and "knitting" when describing how He created us in our mother's womb.[5] You were not thrown together on a whim but were uniquely and carefully crafted by the same Creator who thought the world needed beaches, mountains, puppies, and coffee.

God gave you strengths, and He gave you weaknesses. And while it's opposed to human logic, it's actually not your strengths that make you powerful and your weaknesses that limit you. Both your strengths and your weaknesses, if used as your foundation, will always fail. Not because your personality

1. 2 Corinthians 5:17.
2. Ecclesiastes 3:11.
3. Philippians 3:20.
4. 2 Corinthians 5:21.
5. Psalm 139:13.

is foundationally flawed, but because your personality was never meant to be your foundation.

Christ is your foundation. And when surrendered to Him, your strengths and weaknesses both bring Him glory.

Bottom line: It's only in Him and through Him that you can realize, embrace, and reach all that He has for you. So yes, fight against sin. Fight against your flesh. But you don't have to fight against how He uniquely made you.

You just have to surrender all you are to all He is.

So browse the notes we've written to various personality tendencies on the following pages until you find one (or several!) that fit(s) you. From our hearts to yours, we love you, and we're rooting for you!

To the Perfectionist:

You are made the way you are for a purpose. Your attention to detail and determination to please are gifts when submitted to the authority of God. But what you need to know is that His plan will not change based on your performance. Meaning: You cannot mess up the work that He is doing because something isn't perfect enough yet.

Christ is your foundation. And when surrendered to Him, your strengths and weaknesses both bring Him glory.

Sanctification is a beautiful thing in the life of a believer, but it happens over time and only with the help of God. You will never be perfect enough, which means neither will your life, your home, or your work.

God is after your faithful effort, not your perfect effort. So loosen your grip and give Him yourself, not your perfection. That's what He wants.

To the Overthinker:

Overthinkers make some of the world's greatest problem solvers. You see every detail of a situation and then calculate each and every possible outcome. Your ability to think through so many complicated aspects, believe it or not, is a really amazing skill. However, it's easy to become paralyzed by your brain, which has the ability to transform your valuable skill into a full-fledged hazard.

The good news? You don't even have to turn off your brain to find peace. You just have to know in the depths of your heart Who is in charge. Once you truly understand that yes, the enemy is real, but that God is victorious, and by faith in Jesus your forever is sealed in Him, even the "worst-case scenario" becoming your reality can't shake you. He has you!

Isn't that the best complement to your overthinking, problem-solving brain? Knowing that you are able to solve problems and discern situations without fear of the what-ifs? Because the what-ifs can't happen outside of God's plan for your life!

So it's okay to see them and even to prepare for them, but it is not okay to needlessly and excessively worry over them because there are no what-ifs for God. You don't have to rewire yourself—you couldn't if you tried. You just have to give your brain to the One who created it.

He will use the gift He gave you for His glory and your good. That's a promise.

To the Anxious:

In case no one has ever told you, women who struggle with anxiety are typically more highly aware of their surroundings, which leads them to see others first, and they have a greater level of empathy than most people because they care on a very deep level for their friends and family. If you have always viewed your anxious tendencies as negative, always remember God can do incredible things when we surrender our weaknesses to Him.

Scripture tells us that the very way you are wired is for a purpose, and as much as it may be hard to experience or understand in the moment, trust us when we tell you, God will use your unique situation and suffering to bring himself glory and to make you more like Him . . . if you let Him.

Your love for others and concern for their well-being might make you more anxious, but it can also make you everything this world needs and exactly what Christians are called to be: empathetic, loving, and caring believers, who in their suffering put the needs of others before their own with one goal in mind—to see God glorified. That is how you let Him.

You are more than your anxiety. You are a child of God with an innate ability to feel for the world. Let your feelings move you to action. We pray for your peace, but we also pray that you find the most incredible joy even in your suffering.

To the Discontented:

You do understand that it is absolutely 100 percent okay to want more, don't you? To feel restless or bored is not sin in and of itself. To wake up with a deep desire to change the world or set it on fire is a quality that is found in great leaders. Jesus called us to be world changers and not to sit idly as we wait for His return. There is big important work to be done here on earth and no time to waste.

But . . . (You knew it was coming!) in order for any of those feelings to be more than just feelings, your heart has to be aligned with God's and your desires must be His desires.

If your discontentment drives you to want to change the world so that it will know you, you're in a very dangerous place that may lead you to wasting your life. This world, and everything in it, will pass away. Pursuing what the world can give you will only increase the emptiness inside of you that only God can fill.

If your discontentment drives you to want to change the world so that it will know God, you, our friend, are the best kind of discontented. Get after it! Be faithful where you are. And yes, ask God for more! We're excited for where He will take you and how He will use you! Because with pure ambition, the opportunity doesn't have to look like much for God to do something far bigger than the world expects.

To the One Who Is All or Nothing:

Are you so tired of the constant pendulum swing in your life? In everything you decide to do, are you either all in or all out? Especially in your work and at home, do you fall under the categories of either motivated and driven, or Netflix binging and couch potato-ing?

Guess what? Your extreme behavior, although super frustrating to you, isn't really all that bad. Most likely, you're all or nothing because you're easily motivated, which can be a good quality to have! Until it wears off, which you can guarantee it will do quickly if you have the wrong motivation.

Here's what you have to remember: When Jesus ascended to heaven after His resurrection, He told us that He was giving us something even better than himself. It's crazy to think there could be anything better than having Jesus standing beside you, but that's what He did when He gave us the Holy Spirit, which is Jesus in you.

And this is why that matters for you: Because the Holy Spirit will be your motivator.

He will prompt your passion and excitement every day for the rest of your life if you let Him. He's not here just to convict you when you're wrong and whisper Bible verses when you need help. The Holy Spirit is here to remind you and direct you toward your purpose and calling if you'll only listen to Him. And a woman who understands her purpose and her calling will not be as likely to swing on the pendulum because she will be walking (or more than likely running) with Jesus.

Get off the swing—you're ready to run.

To the Workaholic:

You are disciplined, you are determined, and you are a difference-maker. Not only do you work hard, but you inspire those around you to work hard too. There's so much about the way you're wired that is incredibly admirable.

But here's the thing: Your tendencies to get things done often drive you to self-reliance as your go-to response instead of depending on the Lord. And self-reliance is really an accidental admittance of your perceived self-importance.

Your tunnel vision serves as an incredible asset for whatever you set your mind to. Every organization and every mission needs people like you. But without God as your guardrail, your one-track mind can also create a blind spot for what matters most.

And friend, God created you for so much more than simply getting things done. You will never be one who is too lazy to work His way, but you might allow yourself to get too busy. And too busy and too lazy can both create the same devastating result.

We need people with your drive and ambition bringing a fierce level of commitment for the Gospel to reach our lost world. And while you will no doubt find your way to be one of those who strives for the "ends of the earth," always remember your influence is needed right there in your home, your church, your community, and your work.

Free yourself from the pressure of being the woman who makes everyone wonder how you do it all and embrace the peace that comes when you commit to simply being a woman who depends on God more than herself. Instead of being the woman who is always working, be a woman God can work in.

Because those He can work in, He can work through.

To the Fixer:

You are a natural helper. You're not one to see a problem and complain. You see a problem and you spring into action. In work settings, you're the glue of your organization. There's not much that doesn't find its way to your desk because people know when they need you, you're always there, eager and willing to do whatever you can.

But any problem you can't fix can easily feel personal. So much so that you sometimes fool yourself into believing that you're the problem, even when circumstances are obviously outside of your control. And we say fool yourself because believing you can fix everything means you don't actually see yourself as the problem, but you've started to see yourself as the solution. Even your desire to help can cause trouble when it's not submitted to the authority of Jesus.

Because you're quick to accept the blame, you can also easily get caught in the guilt cycle. Please remember that guilt comes from the enemy, and his goal is to tear you down, tie you to shame, and keep you dwelling in the past. Conviction is completely different. Conviction comes from God, and His goal is to restore you, draw you to repentance, and refocus you on your future. Keep your heart soft to the Holy Spirit's conviction, but do not waste brain space dwelling on the devil's condemnation.

Also, even though you love to help others, you don't like admitting when you need help yourself. Logic tricks you into believing that no one will want your help if you're the one who sometimes needs to be fixed. But there's a reason why God's Word refers to us as "jars of clay."[1] Because this side of heaven, we will constantly need God to mold us, shape us, and correct us to be more like Him.

You will be the helper everyone around you needs when you commit to letting Him fix you on the regular and when you rely on Him to be the real Fixer.

To Every SWHW Woman:

The workplace might be the greatest underutilized mission field believers occupy every day. The mission field isn't a far-off destination, and ministry isn't confined to the walls of the church. The mission field is anywhere a believer goes and ministry is any work a believer does that is submitted to God.

Working His way is not easy, but it is simple. Whenever you find things getting complicated (which is different from difficult!), it's probably because some of that my way is getting mixed in with His way. And you will always be frustrated and exhausted trying to run two races.

Working His way is not easy, but it is simple.

If you can trust God for your eternity, you can trust Him for your right now.

You've got this—because He's got you.

1. 2 Corinthians 4:7–9.

Acknowledgments

To our families: James + Kent, Kennedi + Lizzie, Noah, Cole + Shea, Mom + Dad + every Caldwell, Phoebus, McNatt + Myers: You are our greatest earthly blessings. Thank you for all the coffee runs, random conversations to bounce ideas off of you, calls + texts, offering encouragement or brain breaks (whatever the moment required!) along the way. The way you love and support us spurs us on to run harder after Jesus. Every SWHW project has more purpose as we do life with you. Plus, you bring the joy factor into our days, and we are super grateful God gave us the families He did.

To the SWHW team—Teeny, Erica + Liz: There's so much of each of you here in these chapters. From the graphic design to team meetings that turned into Bible studies + prayer time, we are so grateful for the heart and skill you put in every day to help further the SWHW mission. Thanks for always making our words pretty and grammatically correct, for being smiling faces we can always count on, and for all of the hours you spend behind the scenes selflessly serving the Lord, your family

+ this community. Thanks for sharpening us and leading by example every day.

To our pastors + church families—Bruce Frank + Jamie Caldwell and the support staff + members of Biltmore Church + South Shore Church: We've decided the three words most often used inside SWHW are, "My pastor says . . . " Your commitment to truth strengthens our commitment. We love the local church, and we're so glad you are ours. Thank you for proclaiming and demonstrating the Gospel, for serving us, and for giving us a place to serve.

To the SWHW community: We'll never be able to fully express how much it means to us that you're here. You know that saying no to most things is what allows you to put your yes where it belongs. So the fact that you've said yes to SWHW is seriously such an honor, and we do not take it lightly. We're so grateful for the real conversations we get to have with you and for the way we get to remind one another of what matters most. Most everything in these pages we've said to you first. Thank you for being a safe place (and a fun place!) we can go to share what God is showing us. No matter how annoyed we may be at the internet at any given moment, we'd take ten times the crazy as long as we get you out of the deal. We love you!

To our mentors + friends: You have been there through it all. Through growth and through loss. Through the best days and through the discouraging ones. You've challenged us, you've encouraged us, you've sharpened us, you've served us, and you've strengthened us. Thank you for always being there, even if you're miles away. God uses you on the regular to give us just the reminders we need to keep the main thing the main thing.

To our team at Bethany House: You have been an absolute dream to work with. Thank you for helping us take the mission we've been working toward for years and put it in book form. We are forever grateful for the way you embraced the SWHW mission as your own and brought your expertise to the table to serve us. We love you, and we're so grateful for each of you!

To Somer (from Michelle): I cheated, sorry not sorry. But I can't say thank you to everyone and not say thank you to you. You are the Ann to my Leslie, the Janet to my Michael, the tacos to my sushi and the French fries to my dark chocolate. (I realize now that the last two only make sense to us, and that's okay!) But for real, thank you. I am better in every area of my life because God forced you to be my friend, and you're stuck with me forever, so I'm glad you realized it's easier not to fight it. Thank you for saying yes to serving SWHW. I know you say your job is to simplify (which you do!), but simplicity and clarity go hand-in-hand. The SWHW mission has never been more real and more clear to me—thanks largely to you. Thanks for challenging me + teaching me, encouraging me + making my life more fun + picking out all my outfits too. I love you!

To Michelle (from Somer): Of course you cheated here. Gratitude and generosity are kind of your thing, so I'm not really surprised. M, thank you for constantly and unapologetically forcing me to be brave. Thanks for pulling out of me what I didn't think was there (and didn't necessarily want to be there) and for not letting me quit when I felt unqualified or just annoyed with the world. Your brain is super weird, like super weird—most genius visionary's brains are. But it is one of my greatest honors to translate all of your crazy ideas to the rest of the world who would otherwise struggle to follow you (since you mostly operate both physically + mentally at about 150 mph). Lastly, and I speak on behalf of all us gals out here trying to do this working woman thing God's way, we are immensely grateful to you for being obedient because it is your obedience that led all of us here. So thank you! And I love you too!

Notes

Chapter 1: His Story

1. Timothy J. Keller, *Counterfeit Gods: The Empty Promises of Money, Sex, and Power, and the Only Hope That Matters* (New York: Penguin Books, 2009), 131.

Chapter 2: His Way

1. Elisabeth Elliot, *Discipline: The Glad Surrender* (Grand Rapids, MI: Revell, 2006), 118.
2. Story and quotes shared with permission; name changed to protect confidentiality.
3. Text from Anna.
4. Text from Anna.
5. D.A. Carson, *For the Love of God, Volume 2: A Daily Companion for Discovering the Riches of God's Word* (Wheaton, IL: Crossway Books, 1999), 23.
6. John Piper, "Holiness Is a Race, Not a Prohibition." *DesiringGod.org*, https://www.desiringgod.org/interviews/holiness-is-a-race-not-a-prohibition.

Chapter 4: Know God

1. C.S. Lewis, *Mere Christianity* (New York, NY: HarperOne, 2002), 124.
2. J.I. Packer, *Knowing God* (20th anniversary ed., Downers Grove, IL: InterVarsity Press, 1993), 41.
3. Eric Geiger, *How to Ruin Your Life: and Starting Over When You Do* (Nashville, TN: B&H Publishing Group, 2018), 110.
4. Shared anonymously with permission (emphasis added) by Michelle Myers (@Michellelmyers), Instagram, March 21, 2019, https://www.instagram.com/p/BvRESwoHVwR/?igshid=1tzq5zdj5eewa.

Chapter 5: Obedience

1. Elisabeth Elliot, *Through Gates of Splendor* (Carol Stream, IL: Tyndale Momentum, 1981), 210.

Chapter 6: You

1. This is also the title of a compelling book on the subject by Lisa Whittle, *Jesus Over Everything: Uncomplicating the Daily Struggle to Put Jesus First.*
2. J.D. Greear, *Gaining by Losing: Why the Future Belongs to Churches that Send* (Grand Rapids, MI: Zondervan, 2016), 131.
3. Andy Stanley, (@AndyStanley), "As leaders, we are never responsible for filling someone else's cup. Our responsibility is to empty ours." Twitter, April 2, 2020, 5:54 p.m. https://twitter.com/AndyStanley/status/1245831880320180225.

Chapter 8: Love

1. Warren W. Wiersbe, *On Being a Leader for God* (Ada, MI: Baker Books, 2011), 39.

Chapter 9: Listen

1. Andy Stanley (@AndyStanley), "Leaders who refuse to listen will eventually be surrounded by people who have nothing significant to say," Twitter, August 17, 2011, 9:50 a.m., https://twitter.com/andystanley/status/103841035108630528?lang=en.
2. Dietrich Bonhoeffer, *Life Together: The Classic Exploration of Christian Community* (New York: Harper One, 1954), 97.

Chapter 10: Serve

1. John Piper, "For His Sake and for Your Joy, Go Low," DesiringGod.org, December 17, 2011, https://www.desiringgod.org/messages/for-his-sake-and-for-your-joy-go-low.
2. Angela Mader (@theangelamader), Instagram, February 24, 2020, https://www.instagram.com/p/B8-Ng_KgTlF/?igshid=1946gmb8d46gy.

Chapter 12: Approved

1. AsapSCIENCE, "5 Ways Social Media Is Changing Your Brain," TEDEd video, :22, https://ed.ted.com/best_of_web/qQzsdX2Y#watch.
2. If you invited Christ to be the Lord of your life today, will you email us at hello@sheworksHisway.com to let us know? We'd love to rejoice with you in your decision and follow up with some next steps for you.

Michelle Myers had no idea what started as a Google Hangout at 5 AM with three friends would one day evolve into the nonprofit ministry now known as She Works HIS Way. She's the author of *Famous in Heaven and at Home*, as well as the creator of Network Marketing Nobility and the SWHW Business Tracker. She also serves alongside her husband, James, a pastor at Biltmore Church, and is mom to Noah, Cole, and Shea.

Somer Phoebus is a lead communicator at She Works HIS Way and the creator of Productivity Academy + The 3 Step Planner. She also serves alongside her husband, Kent, a pastor at South Shore Church in Annapolis, MD, and is mom to their two lovely daughters, Kennedi and Ava Liz.

Notes on Working His Way

Notes on Working His Way

Notes on Working His Way

Notes on Working His Way

Notes on Working His Way

Notes on Working His Way

Notes on Working His Way

Notes on Working His Way